Rena

Rena

How to Succeed in
Spite of Life's Challenges

Rena Tarbet
WITH KAREN ANDERSON

LEGACY
COMMUNICATIONS GROUP, INC.
Franklin, Tennessee

Legacy books may be purchased for business or sales promotional use. For information please write: Special Markets Department, Legacy Communications Group, Inc., 251 Second Avenue South, Franklin, Tennessee 37064.

First Printing: July 1998

All Scripture quotes are taken from the New King James Bible, Copyright © 1979,1980,1982, Thomas Nelson, Inc., Publishers. Used by permission.

ISBN 1-880692-32-5

Library of Congress Catalog Card Number: 98-067218

Printed in the United States of America

TABLE OF CONTENTS

DEDICATION

This book is dedicated to my family. First, my devoted parents, Kenneth and Pearl Dack, who gave me the foundation of values, morals and good work ethics from the beginning. And my wonderful husband, Eddie, who shares me with the world without complaining. I truly am blessed by my three wonderful children Jeff, Kim, and Brian, and their spouses, Tracy, Shawn, and Jill. No mother could ask for more caring and attentive offspring. Zak, Tyler, Olivia, and Zoe are the most precious grandkids on this earth and truly the joy of my life. And finally, my sister, Vera, who believes I can do anything and has survived the antics I have gotten her into over the years.

ACKNOWLEDGMENTS

First, I would like to thank my publisher, David Dunham. We started out as acquaintances; now we are friends. David, I have tremendous respect for your expertise and for your humble spirit in sharing that wisdom. You are truly His servant and He is using you in a mighty way.

Karen Anderson, this book has been a God thing with you and I am very much aware of that. You have felt lead by Him since the book's conception and you have thrown your heart into it and spent many a sleepless night. Thank you for helping me put the finishing touches on my story.

How can I ever thank my office manager and assistant, Michele Wong-Ota? She sees me at my best and at my worst and still loves me anyway! I am truly blessed to have you Michele.

The odds are that I would not be alive today if it were not for the medical knowledge and compassionate heart of Dr. Amanullah Khan. He truly is the most dedicated person I know to his profession and to mankind. I am extremely grateful to be his patient and his friend.

When thinking of the people who have been a major influence in my life, I must thank my friend Paul, whose support, encouragement, and belief in me has made a tremendous difference in my life.

Joyce Read spent many hours reading and rereading the manuscript, checking for points I may have forgotten. Thank you, my friend, for your genuine love and concern.

My identical friend, Linda McConnico, loves me unconditionally. We are one spirit in two bodies. Without the nurturing and spiritual strength she generates, I would not be the same person.

My friend, Zig Ziglar has played a major role with his suggestions, drawn from his years of experience. I am very grateful for his input.

If it weren't for Mary Kay Ash—her dream, her vision, and her courage—I would never have had the opportunity for personal growth and thus the training and preparation necessary to endure the obstacles and challenges I've had to face.

Finally, I want to thank my family. They continue to greatly inspire me to want to leave my life's story as a legacy to my grandchildren. Without their love, support, and patience, this book would not have been possible.

FOREWORD

Rena is a book written from the head and heart of Rena Tarbet to your own head and heart, and it will move you emotionally, spiritually, and logically throughout.

This book is loaded with the information and inspiration necessary to help you overcome obstacles and succeed in your life. It offers a balance between winning financially and flourishing at home with your mate and children, and it keeps always before you the spiritual purpose of life on earth, which is eternal victory.

I have never met anyone like Rena Tarbet nor read a book which contained the elements which this one does: overcoming seemingly insurmountable obstacles, living with cancer for many years, undergoing extensive treatments, enduring the pain, the inconvenience, the frustrations, and yes, on occasion, the fears and anxieties that attend the dreaded disease. Rena Tarbet somehow managed to create balance in her topsy-turvy world. Her experiences exemplify the old adage, "You don't drown by falling in water; you drown by staying there." Rena's spirit, excitement, and enthusiasm have endured through her sheer determination to wring as much from her days as she possibly can. I've talked to Rena when she was drained from fighting cancer and yet her faith and enthusiasm were alive and well.

Rena's story has been a classic example of my oft-quoted statement, "You can have everything you want in life if you will just help enough other people get what they want." She has been successful financially because she has helped so many other women become financially successful. She is a successful mother because she has helped her children grow into mature, productive, responsible adults with children of their own, all of whom she unabashedly adores. Through it all, she's been a dedicated wife to her husband, Eddie, and as a couple they have been a beacon on a hill in a time that is seeing the disintegration of the family.

As you read through *Rena*, you will frequently reflect, "If she can get back up off the deck after that, surely I can overcome my challenges." You will often be astounded by her persistence in pursuing her objectives in the face of all the difficulties that confronted her. I believe part of the answer lies in the fact that Rena clearly understands and lives by one of the most important Biblical truths of all: that we are to rejoice in our troubles. Yes, you read it right. Romans 5: 3-4 tells us that problems produce perseverance, perseverance produces character, character produces hope, and hope produces power. Rena Tarbet is a living example.

It's true that the road to the top runs through a series of valleys, and Rena Tarbet has gone through more valleys to get to her mountaintop than anyone else I know. I believe you will love this book. But more importantly, you will love the results the book produces in your life.

Zig Ziglar

Author and Motivational Teacher

A Note from Rena...

Many of you may already be aware of some details of my life's story, and you will doubtless find in this book some references to things with which you are familiar. But since the scope of this book encompasses many events you probably are not aware of, I think it best to begin with a context. So, before I tell you what this book is about, first I want to tell you what this book isn't about!

First, I've battled cancer in various forms and ways for going on twenty-three years. While it's true that this struggle is part of what has made me who I am, and a good chunk of my time is devoted to helping people and their families deal with cancer, this book is not just about fighting cancer.

Second, though I have a business that has become tremendously successful (both in terms of helping people and being highly profitable), and it has brought me a great deal of fulfillment over the years, this book is not just about being successful in business and making a lot of money.

It's true that I have a very close family, even to the extent that my children, their spouses, and my grandchildren all live on the same block as my husband and I—and we're all very happy! I wouldn't be able to see my children and grandchildren frequently if we lived far apart. This way, my grandkids can come over any time and yell, "Rena-Honey, I'm here!" and I can scoop them up and love on them and hear them laugh and squeal with delight. They'll grow up knowing their grandparents—not just knowing *about* their grandparents. Though we are unusually close, this book is not just about the joys of family.

Finally, the Lord has sustained and guided me throughout my life and taught me how to love Him. My whole life has been about acknowledging Him first and being obedient to whatever He wants to do with my life so His plan is fulfilled and He gets the glory. And yet this book isn't just about faith.

So what *is* this book about? It's about all these things and more. Simply, *it's about life*—life that's worth living and enjoying, that is full of hope in a time when much of the world is in despair. Sure, cancer can get us down, business can get us down, struggles with our families can get us down—there is no question life can be difficult. But, my friends, there can still be joy in the journey. Even in the most excruciating circumstances, when difficult times seem to last forever, how we choose to live each day makes all the difference in the world.

Over the years, many people called me "successful." It's true that I've battled cancer and through it developed a deep, rich faith. It's also true that I've built a prosperous business while raising happy, healthy, responsible kids.

But what exactly is "success"? I believe true success is figuring out your personal best, and then setting your sights high and reaching for your goals—and achieving your goals with a heart that is full of joy and laughter.

Obviously, all of us have to figure out what success is for ourselves. But that doesn't mean we have to figure it out *alone*.

My desire is to give you guideposts along the way to help you figure out what success means to you and how to become and stay successful—whatever challenges you may face—while living your life with joy.

Although I certainly can't tell you what tomorrow will bring, I can help you to learn to live today with fullness and contentment so you never have to be afraid of tomorrow.

It's been said, "We may not know what the future holds, but we know Who holds the future." I believe with all my heart that the secret to success lies in understanding the value of who we are and what we are here to accomplish—and for each of us *to be the very best _me_ I can be!*

INTRODUCTION

Not too long ago, I had a chance to observe a young boy whose mother had obviously said he couldn't do something that he desperately wanted to do. The little boy looked his mother in the eye and said, "But that's not fair." She replied right back, "You're absolutely right. Life's not fair... and you'd better get used to it!"

Inside, I applauded that young mother. She was right; life isn't always fair, and the sooner we learn that the better off we are. One of the keys to happiness is realizing that no matter what comes our way in life, it's how we handle it that makes the difference.

Over the past thirty-odd years, I've talked to women all over the world—women of every size, shape, color and style—and no matter where I am, the question I hear over and over again is, "Rena, how in the world do you do it? How do you manage to have a busy, successful career, a happy, secure family, and fight cancer at the same time... all with a great attitude?"

Well, my friends, this book is all about the answer to that question: how to handle life and truly *live* no matter what the circumstances. I want to share with you some of the principles I've discovered in my journey—principles that have led me to a successful business career and sustained me over my 23-year battle with cancer.

My medical history is not that different from that of lots of people, however, how I have handled it is. My background in sales and motivational speaking has taught me the importance of having a positive attitude, of fight, grit, guts, and of making the most of every situation. What I really want to accomplish is to help you understand that you, too, can develop these attributes, that you can train yourself in this same thought process. If we make a habit of this way of thinking, then, with the help of the Lord, we can win. And while we are in the process of winning, we can touch many lives. We can make it a better world in which to live, not only for ourselves but for our children and for all those who come after us.

I'll be the first one to admit I don't have all the answers. I know that sometimes the only way any of us learns something is by attending the "school of hard knocks"! (I sometimes think I'm at the top of the class!) But I do know that God has a purpose in my life. The experiences I've had, especially in my battle with cancer, have shown me that in those difficult times when life didn't seem fair, I could still make choices about how I lived my life. I could let circumstances overwhelm me, or I could "keep on keeping on" and run the race for the prize.

I'm not just talking about battling cancer here. I'm talking about dealing with life in general. Whether you're struggling with being a single parent, working at an unfulfilling job, taking care of aging parents, or simply trying to make a decent living for your family, remember this: it's how we live that makes the difference between waking up in the morning dreading the day and waking up in the morning confident and ready to enjoy today, no matter what happens.

My heart's desire is for you to have a better and more fulfilling life—a life filled not only with material riches but also with emotional and spiritual treasures. I'm willing to share with you some of the most valuable lessons I've learned. But then the ball is in your court. You have to decide whether to take action on what you've learned. The concepts that have meant the most to me over the years are simple, but they are not easy. Easy means "requiring little or no effort." Simple means "easy to understand," though not necessarily easy to put into practice. And I've learned that success most often comes from working hard at things that are simple.

My friends, the quality of our lives depends not on what happens *to* us but on what happens *in* us. As we come to grips with the fact that life is not fair, we find out that bad things do happen to good people, and that we don't always get what we think we deserve.

So how do you make up your mind to be happy in the midst of adversity? How do you "keep on keeping on" when times are tough, losses are great, pain is insurmountable, business is failing, and your friends have let you down time and time again? I know that when you feel frustrated and worried, it's hard not to feel totally alone (especially if your frustration is tinged with a smidgen of self-pity). You may not even have the strength or the energy to cry out to the Lord. Besides, occasionally you're not even sure whether you want to! After all, sometimes you can get a little bit angry with Him for allowing you to get into this mess in the first place!

Begin by understanding that happiness and contentment do not depend on outward circumstances. As Abe Lincoln once said, "A man is as happy as he makes up his mind to be." Someone once asked me that if I had the choice, wouldn't I rather have things be easy? My answer was an emphatic, "No!" Because when things come to us easily, we often don't appreciate them. There are many things in life I've come to appreciate precisely because they have been hard won.

If I had only one wish today, I would truly wish to live to be three thousand years old! When I read the Old Testament, I'm envious of those folks who lived eight or nine hundred years. Gosh, I'd love that—because I know whenever the Lord comes to get me, *I ain't gonna be through!* So I do everything fast—I talk fast, walk fast, think fast, work fast, play fast—I do everything just as fast as I can. I want to get as much as possible crammed into my life! That is part of my style.

Now, just so you don't confuse my "style" with my message, I want to be perfectly up front with you: I teach with "tough love." I do not apologize for that. I raised my family with tough love, I built my business on tough love, and I believe in tough love. Anytime we do something for people that they are capable of doing for themselves, we are doing them an injustice.

If a baby crawls under the table, raises his head and bumps it, it's natural to want to protect his head, pull him out, and kiss his sweet, little noggin. But if he crawls back under the table and hits his head again, and we drag him back out and kiss him again, that child will never learn how to duck his head and back out by himself.

If you dress your children day after day, they don't learn to distinguish their right from left foot, inside from outside, or front from back. When you establish a pattern of doing everything for them (because you love them) what will happen when they're older? When they become teenagers, they will probably expect you to pay their traffic tickets; after all, you still love them, don't you? In social work terms, we call that being an 'enabler.'

You see, many times we love our family and friends so much that we tend to want to protect them. Sometimes, we want more for them than they want for themselves. If we're not careful we can end up trying to make it happen for them. But even if our hearts and our motives are right, we still end up doing those we love an injustice because they never learn to do it for themselves. This disservice will haunt them all their lives.

So, yes, I'll be tough on you. I may even sound harsh at times. But my goal is to help you to be the very best "you" you can be. We have a responsibility to God to be our very best. We are His greatest creation, and His greatest gift to us is life. What we do with that life is our gift back to Him.

But here's the encouraging news. Even when life is hard, and there isn't anyone there to kiss you when you've bumped your head, one of the best ways I've found to cope with life is simply to laugh. Yes, just laugh. Let's face it, we all know that life's hard and that bad things happen. But the good Lord has given us the wonderful gift of laughter. And here's the best news of all: you can *learn* to laugh and see the lighter side of life. We weren't born comedians, but we can create in ourselves a new way of looking at situations and new ways to respond, and in the end we are happier for it, and we often can even live longer—just because we have laughed.

However, knowing this doesn't help you unless you use it. Remember, it's not what we know, it's what we *do* with what we know. Knowledge, talent, and ability profit us little if we don't take action. Most of us want to do well, to be winners—and yes, the people I admire most in this life are winners. People say, "It doesn't matter whether you win or lose, it's how you play the game." Well, I think that is a bunch of hooey! If it didn't matter whether we won or lost, we wouldn't have scoreboards!

I believe we must all play to win and give it all we've got. But here's where the difference in true winners comes in: true winners understand that even if they don't win, it's still ok, because they know they gave it their *very* best.

CHAPTER I

~ ~

Strength in Weakness

"Brethren, I do not count myself to have apprehended; but one thing I do, forgetting those things which are behind and reaching forward to those things which are ahead, I press toward the goal for the prize of the upward call of God in Christ Jesus."

Phil. 3:13 (NKJV)

Little did I know that at age thirty-two I would be diagnosed with breast cancer.

It was 1975. My life at the time was what I would call pretty normal. I was a full-time mom with a part-time career. I had two boys and a girl ages thirteen, eleven, and nine who were into all the things that kids do: karate, baseball, piano, ballet, and whatever else they could sign up for. My husband Eddie was a full-time social worker who placed abused, neglected, and abandoned children into healthy homes.

In those days, you couldn't do much on a social worker's income, and I wanted my kids to have the opportunity to play sports and have some of the nicer things in life. Eddie was gifted in his work, and I didn't want him to have to sacrifice the job he loved. So I became an independent beauty consultant with Mary Kay Cosmetics as a way to supplement our family income, which was great for me since I was able to work my hours around my kids' schedules. After three years, I became a Sales Director (a leadership position in Mary Kay). I was able to stay home, work part-time, and be a full-time mom. All in all, I'd say we were a pretty typical family.

Then one night, while doing a self-exam on my breast, I felt a lump. Back then there wasn't an emphasis on self-examination, so it was unusual that I found it. I had come in from a skin care class, undressed, and gone to bed. I was just lying there when I felt a bump under my left arm, and there it was! My husband had already gone to sleep, and I woke him up and said, "Oh my gosh, feel this," and there was a lump about the size of a pea.

Now Eddie is a very calm person, and he said, "Well, I'm sure it's nothing. Don't worry about it, we'll get it checked." In the morning, I immediately called my gynecologist, who also said, "I'm sure there is nothing to it, but come on in and let me look at it." When he had finished examining me, he called and scheduled a surgeon to look at it the next day, which was Saturday. That was my first red flag. I knew that surgeons did not see you on Saturdays. Yet, after I saw the surgeon, I began to relax, since he also thought it was nothing. While I was there, the surgeon ran two tests: a needle biopsy and a mammogram, both of which came back negative.

Even though the tests were negative, however, everyone agreed that the lump should come out, so they scheduled me for surgery. In fact, the doctors were so confident that the lump was benign that I didn't even sign a release. That morning Eddie went with me as I checked into the hospital for my minor surgery. This would only be a small lumpectomy, so I didn't even bother to call my parents, since I knew they would worry regardless of how minor the procedure was. But when the surgeon got in there, he was shocked at what he found. He could tell by looking at the lump that it was malignant.

As I said, since none of us expected the lump to be malignant, I hadn't signed a release for a mastectomy. The doctor came into the waiting room and asked Eddie to make the decision: should they wake me up and tell me I needed a mastectomy, give me a day or two to adjust psychologically, and then put me back under for surgery, or should they go ahead and do the mastectomy while I was already under the anesthesia?

Eddie chose the second option and signed the release. He knew me well enough to know that I would have wanted to go ahead with the surgery. Eddie also knew I had confidence in my doctor, and that if my doctor had come in and said, "Rena, we've got to amputate your arm in order for you to live," I'd have said, "Let's do it."

When I woke up, my doctor was standing on one side of my hospital bed, my husband was standing on the other side, and one of my very best friends was standing there with them. They were all crying, including the doctor. He just kept saying, "I'm so sorry, I'm so sorry."

I went into surgery thinking I would have a lump removed and woke up to find I'd had my full breast removed. Needless to say, I was in shock. But when I thought about it, I realized that I had not lost anything vital to my existence, so I moved on from that stage quickly. At least they had removed the cancer successfully.

Now, I only have two stages of response to difficult situations: shock and fight. That's how I handle life. Yes, I was in shock, but then I immediately moved on and thought, "This is okay. I can do with one boob what most people do with two, thank you very much!"

During my recuperation, I had my Mary Kay Cosmetics work brought from home, and I set up my "office" in my hospital room. I wasn't about to sit around doing nothing but thinking about my loss. I had my Rolodex and my phone, and I went right on working!

One of the things I thoroughly enjoy in my role as Sales Director is being an encourager: someone who'll stand beside you and tell you over and over again, "You can do it!" I take my role very seriously because I know how much support helps people achieve success, and I knew many people were depending on me.

One day I was on the phone giving one of my "Rah, rah! You can do it!" pep calls from my hospital bed when one of the young doctors walked into my room. I was my usual self: in high speed, in high gear, talking fast, and cheering someone on. The doctor looked at me and said, "You're on something. What are you taking?" He thought I was taking some kind of drugs on the side!

I said, "I'm not on anything," but he made me hold my hand out steadily to prove I wasn't high on some drug! I looked him square in the eye and said, "You don't seem to understand. I've got places to go, things to do, and people to see.

You see, I had a choice to make. I could sit there, recuperate, and do nothing, or I could sit there, recuperate, and do something *productive* with my time. Wasting time doing nothing didn't make sense to me. After all, it didn't hurt my breast to talk on the phone!

I knew what I needed to do. I had to concentrate on my daily goals and work very hard at being happy. I refused to allow myself to be down for any length of time. I've found that when we have something to look forward to, we stay more positive and motivated. If we don't have anything already, we need to create something. We need to realize we are as happy or as sad as we choose to be and as we make up our minds to be.

One day when my doctor was making his rounds, I broached the subject of the possibility of reconstructive breast surgery.

My doctor at the time was an elderly man and from the "old school." He said that having reconstructive surgery after breast cancer was like smoking after you've been diagnosed with lung cancer. He simply said, "It's stupid; don't do it."

Since I was a married woman and wasn't out trying to impress some young man, I thought it through and decided it really wasn't a big deal. I was very secure in my husband's love for me; Eddie had always been totally supportive through the ordeal, so I didn't have reconstructive surgery.

After I was released from the hospital, I went home and breathed a sigh of relief. My ordeal was over. They had "gotten it all." There wasn't any follow-up therapy. The prevailing school of thought for treatment at that time was simply to cut out the specific area of the cancer as well as all the areas surrounding it. That was it.

In the spring of 1979, approximately four years after my surgery, I again began to think about the possibility of breast reconstructive surgery. Although I had a healthy self-esteem and was very secure, I still wondered if I would feel better with reconstruction. I decided to see whether I was a candidate. My mastectomy had been a "radical": they had taken all the muscle, sweat glands, nerves and lymph nodes—the whole enchilada. I wasn't sure whether I would even qualify for breast reconstruction.

I scheduled a breast reconstruction consultation with a highly recommended plastic surgeon in San Antonio, Texas. After his examination, he came in to talk with me and told me the last thing I expected to hear: the cancer was in my other breast.

My reaction was the same as before: shock and fight. Only this time I said to the doctor, "If we need to do a second mastectomy, fine. But figure out a way to work in the reconstruction, too."

So in 1979, I had four surgeries: another mastectomy and three breast reconstructions. As with the first time, I didn't have any follow-up therapy. But I was back to "normal." They had taken all the cancer, and I had two breasts back.

In the meantime, my career was really starting to take off. My husband and kids were happy, and I was happy.

The next spring, in 1980, I went for my routine check-up only to find that the cancer had now spread to my bones. Again, I had to go into my routine of shock and fight.

By this time, my family and I were used to the word "cancer." But we were not used to the word "chemotherapy." It was a whole new fear for all of us. The less you know about something, the scarier it is, and at that time I had no knowledge about chemotherapy. It was *very* scary.

Although my doctor in Dallas said I needed to start treatment immediately, I decided to check out my options for where to get that treatment before I began.

I researched hospitals in the southwest to find out which had the best reputation for successful treatment of cancer using chemotherapy. I wanted to find the hospital where I would have the best chance of eliminating this now too familiar problem.

Taking the time to investigate hospitals may sound strange, but one of the things I've found over the years is that people who are in shock all too frequently don't participate in the decisions about their treatment. They simply do what they are told. It's easy to understand why. When you hear that cancer has invaded your body, it's natural to feel totally out of control. Things are happening, and there seems to be no way to stop them. It doesn't feel as if there are options. But I've found there are *always* options. They might not be the greatest, but they are always there. So I did my homework and found that the M.D. Anderson Cancer Research Center was the best cancer center in the southwest, and I wanted the very best. That was the good news.

The bad news was that M.D. Anderson was in Houston, and I lived in the Dallas-Ft. Worth area, about 250 miles away. But that didn't stop me! I simply flew (by myself) from the Dallas airport to Houston once every three weeks to get my treatments. I left my house at 6:00 a.m., flew to Houston, had my chemotherapy treatments, caught a 7:00 p.m. plane back to Dallas, and was home by 9:00. (My goal was to be back on a plane by the end of the day and to get home before I started throwing up!) In all the time I went for treatment, I only had to stay overnight twice. I did this every three weeks for a year.

Now it may seem unusual to some people, but going to Houston by myself was important to me. I know if I had a friend who was in a similar position, I'd want to be with her to encourage her, hold her hand, and tell her to hang in there. But I knew I needed to be by myself. If I wanted to cry, I could cry. If I wanted to sit and think, meditate, or just "vege out," I could do it. My friends loved me and would have done anything for me, but it was important for me to have that time to regroup. In the course of my treatment, I went alone every time but twice (Eddie went with me once and my sister-in-law went with me once). I'm sure a psychologist would have had a field day with me, but I knew what I had to do and what was best for me.

At the hospital, my day began at the first "station," where I weighed in and had my vital signs taken. Then I went to the next station for blood work. Finally I saw the doctor and got hooked up on chemotherapy. Let me explain what "hooked up" means.

I received my chemotherapy through a pump that I carried around with me. Today the pumps are so streamlined you just stick them in your bra and go about your business, but back then, in order to pump a continuous infusion of the medication over a four-day period, you had to carry around this big old contraption held in something like a book satchel.

The pump served two purposes: first, it saved the veins, which otherwise tend to weaken and explode over time, and second, it was supposed to keep you from being quite so sick, since the medication was administered in a slow drip infusion rather than a one-shot whammy. On the other hand, it required fresh bandaging every day, including flushing with saline. But as inconvenient as this sounds, it soon became a way of life and part of my daily routine of personal hygiene.

I looked perfectly normal, and I wore a jacket or something over my satchel so that anybody seated by me in the plane would never know the difference.

Since I've always been a "people person," every now and then I tested the waters just to see how people would react. I'll never forget the response I got one time while on an airplane.

I was seated by a young businessman, and we had gotten into a nice conversation on our one-hour flight from Houston to Dallas. He was as warm and friendly as he could be. He asked what I had been doing in Houston. When I told him I was getting cancer treatments and wearing a chemotherapy pump, suddenly his demeanor changed. He pulled back and withdrew. It was as if someone had flipped a switch!

I realized a valuable lesson that day. I didn't take his behavior personally because I knew from experience that sometimes, when people don't understand something, they get uncomfortable and even afraid. But I learned that when I set the tone and looked "normal," people treated me normally.

I hate to admit it, but looking normal for me always meant that I carried around a few "extra" pounds! I've had to watch my weight all my life. I'm one of those unfortunate people who do not have a "fast" metabolism, and I tend to store fat rather than burn it. But with heavy-duty chemotherapy, you'd think the pounds would have been dropping off my body. I figured if I was going to suffer through chemotherapy, at least I'd be thin. Wrong!

One day I said to my doctor, "Okay, where's the skinny body? I thought at least I'd get one good thing out of this disease." He looked at me with tenderness in his eyes and said,

"Rena, you've been looking at all the thin people in the waiting room, haven't you?" I said, "Yes, I have." He paused for a moment and said words that touched my heart, "Rena, those people are dying of cancer—you're living with it."

Those touching words became my anchor in the storm on the days that were really tough.

There came a point when the doctors began to think the chemotherapy wasn't as effective as it should have been. They decided I needed radiation. Fortunately, I was able to get my radiation administered locally in Ft. Worth, so I was delighted I didn't have to fly to Houston!

The game plan was that I would receive twenty rounds of radiation treatments to my breastbone over the course of a month—one round every day, five days a week, for four weeks. At the end of the month I'd go back to M.D. Anderson and return for more chemotherapy.

It was during one of the radiation treatments that a radiologist said to me, "Mrs. Tarbet, I don't know how you're standing up and walking around. Your breastbone looks like a piece of Swiss cheese." It was quite a shock to hear that my bones were full of *holes!* Besides being very unprofessional, his words devastated me emotionally.

But I had recently seen a cartoon of a turkey with a boot on his head and a defeated look on its face with the caption, "Don't let the turkeys get you down!" I thought, "Dadgummit, I'm not going to let that turkey get me down!" That is not to say that I didn't cry—I did—but not for long! Remember, I am driven by goals, and I chose to press on to meet my goals rather than let some inconsiderate young doctor ruin my day.

As soon as my radiation was finished, I went back to chemotherapy to try out a new "recipe." Chemo, in layman's terms, is like mixing a recipe: a half a cup of this, a fourth a cup of that, and a little pinch of something else. Doctors make up the formula they feel your body will most likely respond to. Once again, I began a new formula to see how it would work.

During this period, a dear friend of mine came over to my house to have a cup of coffee and visit. While we were talking, she got a strange look on her face and said, "Rena, may I ask you a rather odd question?" I said, "Of course. You know you can. What is it?"

"If I made the appointment, would you go to a nutritionist?" she asked with a hopeful look on her face. I thought for a moment and replied, "A nutritionist... sure. I don't see why not."

About a week later, I went to see a wonderful gentleman in Arlington, Texas, who believed that nutrition, not chemotherapy, was the best way to treat cancer. I discovered that many holistic doctors, naturopaths and doctors of osteopathic medicine feel that way. He assured me that nutrition was the only way to beat my cancer. He wanted to run some tests, one of which was a hair analysis.

Now getting a sample of my hair practically meant shaving me bald, since the hair I'd lost during chemotherapy had grown back only about an eighth of an inch in the six weeks I'd been on radiation. My eyes filled up with tears, and I said, "I'll have to think about that. I can't make a snap decision." That was at 9:00 a.m.

Later that morning, I had a follow-up appointment with a local oncologist who had treated me a few weeks earlier for a staph infection. When I saw him, I told him about the nutritionist and his recommendations.

After listening intently, the oncologist shook his finger in my face and said point blank, "Without chemotherapy you will die."

CHAPTER 2

Two Steps Forward, One Step Back

I remember leaving the oncologist's office with tears rolling down my cheeks. I cried and prayed all the way home. I said, "Ok, God, you're going to have to help me. One doctor is saying I'll die if I take chemotherapy, and the other doctor's saying I'll die if I don't take it. I just don't know what to do. Please help me. Give me a sign so I'll know what to do."

When I got home, I stopped at the mailbox, and in it, to my surprise, was an article about nutrition. Back then, I was the number one Sales Director in Mary Kay, and because of that, I was very well known, so it was not unusual to find my mailbox crammed full of herbs, tapes, music, onions to tie around my neck, handkerchiefs anointed with oil, and many other gifts. I think I received a copy of nearly every book and every tape out there! Even though I didn't necessarily agree with everything they said, I deeply appreciated each and every one as a gesture of care and concern. I felt loved by so many people in our wonderful company, and I knew the gifts were all sincere, from the heart.

Since I had already received a book from one of the doctors referenced in the article, I fished the book out of my pile, crawled into bed, and spent the rest of the day reading about nutrition. This book confirmed everything that the nutritionist had told me earlier in the day. I said to myself, "Here is my sign." I called the nutritionist and said, "I'll be in first thing in the morning for you to shave my head."

When the tests were completed, the nutritionist said, "I can make you only one promise: you'll live longer without chemotherapy than you will with it."

I decided to try a six-month treatment plan based strictly on nutrition. At the end of that time I would go back to M. D. Anderson, have all my tests and lab work repeated, and then re-evaluate my condition. When I knew whether or not I had progressed, I would make my next decision.

The nutritionist gave me seven food no-no's (I've read a squillion books since then, and they all give you the same seven): no beef, pork, sugar, salt, white flour, caffeine or dairy products. When I first heard the list I thought I'd end up dying of starvation! But once I got into my new diet, it really wasn't all that bad. I primarily ate steamed vegetables, fresh salads, fresh fruit, and whole grains, and I started drinking tons of water. For the next six months, not one thing that wasn't "legal" crossed my lips. I mean, if someone was baking a cake, I didn't even lick the spoon!

Was I tempted to cheat? *Absolutely not!* You see, I was scared, and when you're scared, you're very obedient.

Toward the end of the six months, my dear friend and mentor Mary Kay got a horrible case of shingles and was hospitalized in Dallas. One day she called and said, "Rena, I'd love to have you visit me. Would you mind coming over? I'm really lonely."

Well, of course, I *immediately* dropped everything and went to see her!

I'll bet I hadn't been in her room five minutes when her doctor "just happened" to come by on his rounds. Dr. Khan (a Pakistani by birth) is a brilliant, compassionate human being, and Mary Kay has always had the highest respect for him. After she introduced me to Dr. Khan she said in her sweet, precious way, "You know, I've been telling Dr. Khan about you and your situation, but I can't explain it like you can, Rena. Would you tell him about it?"

So I gave Dr. Khan the five-minute *Reader's Digest* version of my medical history up to, and including, my new nutritional program. I told him it was nearly time to get my tests updated to see how I was progressing. Dr. Khan surprised me and asked, "Would you mind doing your tests here?" I said, "Sure. Why not?" (Flying to Houston was not my favorite thing to do anyway!)

I completed a full battery of tests: CAT scans, bone scans, MRI's, blood work, X- rays, and just about every test they could run. When the results were all in, Dr. Khan's office called to schedule a consultation. That consultation became a milestone in my life.

We were sitting in his hospital office. Dr. Khan was on his side of the desk, and I was on the other. In his soft-spoken, compassionate manner he looked at me and said, "How against chemotherapy are you?"

I didn't even blink my eyes. I immediately replied, *"Very!"* I had been under the nutritionist's care for six months, and I was convinced I would <u>never</u> go back on chemotherapy!

Dr. Khan looked me straight in the eye and said, "Rena, we need to talk."

He pulled out a pile of papers and handed them to me. My tests showed that I had three new tumors: one in my skull, one in my left shoulder, and one in my lower back.

I felt as if a truck had run over me. When what he was saying started to sink in (I thought he was trying to lure me back to chemotherapy, but I was already sold on nutrition—or rather on non-chemotherapy) I became frightened as I had never been frightened before.

It's been said that fear brings out an unusual side in people, and it did in me that day. I remember saying to him with an arrogant tone, "Dr. Khan, you can talk all you want—but I'm a better salesperson than you!" I knew I could out-talk him any day of the week!

Still he was very kind, very gentle and very patient. While explaining my situation, he said, "Rena, I'm not asking you to abandon your nutrition program. In fact, I want you to continue your nutrition. But the reality is, we've got to get back on chemo."

Dr. Khan went on to say, "I believe good nutrition is very important in preventing cancer, but you can't close the gate after the cows are out. Statistics show that only five percent of breast cancer is from genetics: the rest results primarily from smoking and diet. I agree that good nutrition is essential to preventing cancer, but good nutrition won't kill the bad cancer cells that are already there. We need to bring out the 'big guns' to do that. If we don't, the cancer will continue to grow, and there will be no hope."

Because of Dr. Khan's gentle, wise spirit and his extraordinary knowledge of cancer, I listened and became his patient. Thinking about it later, I realized that if Dr. Khan had been cocky or condescending, I would've walked out the door right then. That would've been a tragic mistake.

Under Dr. Khan's care, I had chemotherapy treatment every three weeks for the next five years. That made a total of six years of chemotherapy with only one six-month break. And finally, after all that time, we found we had the cancer in remission. I say "we" because it truly was a team effort. And I thank God that Dr. Khan was the best salesperson!

I can remember the day I received the news of my remission as if it were yesterday. When Dr. Khan said, "We're done, Rena. No more chemotherapy," I wanted to shout it from the rooftops! I wanted to announce it on the radio and on television and drive up and down the freeways of Dallas with a megaphone!

I wanted to hire an airplane and write it in the sky! I was just so excited!

I thought the whole world would be excited with me, especially the people who were closest to me. I learned a difficult lesson that day, however. The people who loved me the most were the first to say, "Well, how long do they think this remission will last?" or "What are the odds that you'll make it past five years?" and so forth. Despite being very thick-skinned, before the day was over I was devastated.

I came home, took off my wig, eyelashes and makeup, removed my contacts, and went to bed. I cried and cried and cried.

Please don't misunderstand. My dear friends were not intentionally trying to hurt me. In fact, I know it was just the opposite. Their intent was to protect me (and themselves as well) from false hope. I understood this. Nevertheless, their hopelessness was very painful. But as I lay on my bed, all of a sudden that old "Tarbet" spunk kicked in! It started at my feet and moved right up to my head. I thought, "I'll be dadgummed if anyone's going to rain on my parade!" I got out of my bed, put myself back together and went out to take on the world again.

I was in remission for ten years. In the world of cancer, when you've been in remission for five years, it's an achievement worth talking about. When you make ten years you think, "It's finally over. I'll never have to deal with this again." The tenth anniversary of my remission was in May 1996.

One month later, cancer reared its ugly head again.

At the time, nothing seemed out of the ordinary. I was going in for regular checkups and feeling great. But then I started having some "female" problems, so the doctor decided to run some additional tests, given my previous history. They ran "the usual"—bone scans, liver scans, CAT scans, MRIs, etc.—I got the works.

They did a uterine biopsy, and even though it came back benign, I had a hysterectomy to prevent uterine cancer from developing. After all the tests and the surgery, I received the good news that all of my female parts had a clean bill of health.

But there was bad news, too: they discovered more cancer in my skull. Dr. Khan told me later, "Rena, had we been fighting cancer in both places, it would've been like playing two different ball games on the same field. We would not have had good odds."

As the saying goes, there are two ways to look at a glass: half empty or half full. I accepted this news as another example of a blessing in disguise—we didn't have to battle cancer in my skull *and* my female parts!

FILLING IN THE GAPS

The skull is composed of basically two layers of bone with squishy stuff in between. (I'm sure the medical world would love my description!) The inner layer next to my brain is intact. The outer layer is totally gone, eaten away from the crown of my head to the nape of my neck. Surprisingly, I've never had problems with headaches. It's amazing how God has given the human body an extraordinary ability to bounce back. Although it may take years, bone actually fills itself back in!

When people ask, "How are you? What's happening with your treatments?" it's hard to describe. I can't say something simple like, "I had a tumor the size of a grapefruit, and now it's down to the size of an egg," because it literally takes *years* for bone to fill back in.

So when I am asked how my skull is, I just say, "We're closing the gaps, one by one." We are making progress, slowly but surely, toward getting the malignant cells under control.

People are often curious about what happens when you lose your hair. Every time I've had chemotherapy, my hair has fallen out. Not just some of it—*all* my hair has fallen out! All types of chemotherapy don't cause you to lose your hair, but certain ones do, without exception, on the fourteenth day of treatment.

I'll never forget the first time I lost my hair. I was leaving the next day on a trip to Spain. My entire family gathered around the dining room table, and together we plucked out clumps of hair just like you would pluck a chicken.

My daughter Kim, the only girl and fifteen at the time, was the most emotional.

As we sat there and pulled my hair all out, she ran into the kitchen and got a baggie to put it in. Great clumps of hair were falling out with every stroke of the brush. With tears streaming down her face, Kim looked at me and said, "Mommy, I love you anyway!" We held each other and cried together.

I have to admit, seeing yourself totally bald is tough. There is really no way to prepare yourself for the experience. I thought I would be ready simply because I knew it was going to happen, but it was a shock nevertheless. In the months that followed, my family and I worked out a "secret code" of sorts. When the boys came home with a friend after school, they would hit the downstairs door and yell, "Mom, I'm home, and I have a friend with me."

That was my cue. If I didn't have my hair on, I had to grab my wig and quickly put it on, or run upstairs and hide, or else be caught bald! Either of the first two options was fine; I just didn't want to come downstairs bald as a billiard ball and shock one of the boys' friends!

One of things that made me so secure in those difficult times was that my kids loved me so much that they didn't mind bringing their friends home to a bald mother! In fact, our house always had tons of kids running through it, sometimes when I least expected them! But it was always okay with me because I wanted my kids to feel as if their home was no different from anybody else's. As my youngest son Brian once said, "Tommy's mom had a car wreck, Paul's mom broke her arm, and my mom had cancer; it's no big deal." My kids just took it in stride.

When I lost my hair, Kim, in her innocence, found just the right words when she said, "Mommy, I love you anyway!" Her sweet words became another anchor for me.

The next day I left on my trip to Spain. Now there is something you need to know about this trip to fully understand just how supportive and encouraging Kim was, and what a significant difference that made for me.

The trip to Spain was a promotional trip other top performers and I had won. Mary Kay is the best company there is when it comes to "carrots-on-a-stick" motivation. This trip was a reward to the top achievers. In other words, I was with some of the most talented and successful women in business today, not to mention some of the most beautiful! But one of the things I learned early on from Mary Kay, the lady herself, was that "beauty is both what's on the inside as well as what's on the outside."

There's a scene at the end of the movie, *The Wizard of Oz*, that is one of my favorites. The Old Professor (a.k.a. the Wizard) is making presentations to the Lion, Scarecrow and Tin Man. He takes out a chain with a large heart hanging on it and hands it to the Tin Man. The wise old Wizard says, "Hearts will never be practical until they can be made unbreakable. So remember, my sentimental friend, a heart is not judged by how much you love, but by how much you are loved by others."

Now, intellectually I knew that was true, but at the time I was feeling far from beautiful. But then I began to reflect on the love of my family. As Kim sat with me while I tried on my new wig the night before I left, I knew for a fact that she loved me with all her heart, hair or no hair. I thought about Eddie's devotion to me, as well. I said to myself, "Tarbet, you know better than to compare yourself to other people. You can choose to look at this as being the worst situation you've ever been in, or you can choose to look at this as a golden opportunity to understand what true beauty is all about."

The decision was easy. Beauty and self-esteem are all about being happy with who you are in whatever situation you're in. Knowing I am truly loved for who I am by the people I treasure most gives me the best feeling in the world.

After I completed the first six years of chemotherapy, my hair finally started to grow back. At first it was only about a quarter of an inch of fuzz, but then it started filling in like real hair! Pretty soon I could go without my wig, and I felt wonderfully free.

When I started thirty rounds of radiation to my skull in June of 1996, once again, out came my hair. It appears now that the radiation treatments may have destroyed my hair follicles, so it's likely I may never have hair again. But I choose to look at the glass as half full. Although I may be wearing a wig for the rest of my life, there certainly could be worse things. At least I won't ever have a bad hair day!

SHIFTING GEARS... AGAIN

I completed the radiation in July 1996 and started chemotherapy, which I took for the next sixteen months. In October 1997, I once again went in for a routine check-up. I was close to finishing my chemotherapy and was feeling fine. My dear friend Dr. Khan had the results of my tests on his desk. He said quietly, "Rena, we need to talk. The latest tests show that there is a spot of cancer on your spine. The chemotherapy we are using is not strong enough. We need to switch to a much stronger type."

"Not again!" I thought. But just as before, I went into my two stages: shock and fight. That first night was rough. I just couldn't believe it had spread. But I had to make a choice. I could give up and say I was too tired to keep trying, or I could get up and go at it again.

My choice: go for it! I have too much I want to live for. I believe God is not through with me yet! I still want to touch so many lives, help people realize they have the God-given ability to become anything they want, and teach them to learn and grow from every experience—especially the ones that don't turn out the way we want them to.

Giving up simply isn't an option.

CHAPTER 3

Fighting the F-E-A-R Battle

In crises, most people go though a number of stages before they are ready to deal with what has happened to them: they typically go from shock to denial to anger to blaming God (or asking, "Why me?"), and finally acceptance. Now, by acceptance I don't mean "I'm going to take this lying down," but rather "I really do have a problem, and let's deal with it."

Shock, in my opinion, is the toughest of all the stages. We all have difficulty in dealing with the unexpected, especially when it is of a negative nature. When we first hear we have cancer, we often react negatively due to our lack of knowledge and understanding. We immediately associate cancer and death as synonymous. I think the number one emotion we feel is fear.

Fear is an emotion of alarm, of agitation. It's caused by the expectation or realization of danger. It's not necessarily dependent on the facts of a situation, but rather on how we perceive it to be. Fear is oftentimes "False Evidence Appearing Real:" F-E-A-R. Two important choices now present themselves: we can remain in a state of fear and panic, or we can fight to stay in control. If we avoid falling apart, we make it easier for our family, our friends, and ourselves. It's the old theory of "fake it to make it." Act like the person you want to become in order to become that person. It's self talk—you talk it, you act it.

Act as if you are enthusiastic until finally you *are* enthusiastic. Pretty soon you're no longer pretending.

Actually, I like to talk to myself. In fact, I even answer myself occasionally. It's just when you find yourself saying, "Huh?" to your own questions that you have a problem! While talking to myself during the good times, I often record my thoughts in written form. On the tough days, I'm able to go back and reread those thoughts. This simple practice has been a tremendous source of strength to me.

Another thing I've found is that when we're afraid of a situation, if we just take the first step toward whatever it is we fear, then God will take us the rest of the way. A positive attitude has proven to be essential to me regardless of circumstances or conditions. We have to take life one day at a time. That is the way the Good Lord gives it to us, and that is the way we have to live it, with our chin up and our faith in God's providence intact.

When I was in shock from discovering my cancer, probably the greatest fear I had to deal with was the fear of the unknown. Was I going to live? How long would it last? Could I live a normal life? That fear comes from our tendency to think in terms of security. We are taught to look for guarantees. Not knowing what's going to happen can produce some of the greatest fears in the whole world.

With the passing of time, my fear gradually began to fade. It was certainly never totally gone, however. It etched a certain vulnerability in me that left a visible pain, a loss, and a sorrow. I knew that without a dream there was no reason to work. In turn, unless I worked there was no use in dreaming. I felt as if I was in a Catch-22. I wanted to dream, set goals, move ahead and think long range, but at the same time I was afraid. That old fear of the unknown haunted me.

One thing that helped me get through the tough times was knowing that there were others who had struggled with the same questions and conquered their fears. I wanted to learn from their experiences. They shared with me what they did to get past their fear, even though many of their situations were not exactly like mine. Listening and asking questions became powerful tools for disarming my fear.

A vital ingredient to healing the wounds of fear is simply time. We live in an age of instant gratification—instant coffee, instant tea, instant microwaves and instant everything. We often forget the wise words of Hippocrates, "Healing is a matter of time." Actually, the word "therapy" means a process, a prolonged period of recovery for both the mind and the body. Although there are times when God does heal instantly, miraculously, and unexplainably, such miracles are rare. More often than not, it takes time to heal, to recover under the care of a competent physician. This is especially true for those with a background of emotional trauma.

Time also gives us the opportunity to increase our awareness. The better we understand a situation, the better we are able to deal with it.

I've also found that as knowledge is gained and awareness increases, many people move from shock to the second stage, denial. Denial is where we tend to use the "ostrich approach": we bury our heads in the sand, deny the facts, and hope the problem will go away. Intellectually we know this approach won't work, but emotionally this is exactly what we do. But denying the facts doesn't make them any less real.

I believe God helps those who help themselves. We must work as though everything depends upon us and pray as though everything depends upon God. We must force ourselves to look at our options, accept the facts, weigh the pros and cons, and then make the most intelligent decision we can. Once we've gathered the facts and information, it is time to act. It all comes back to making a choice.

Freedom, along with the ability to make choices, is a precious gift from God. I believe it's the most valuable gift we've been given next to life itself. Usually the denial stage doesn't last long; problems have a way of finding closure with or without our help. We soon either accept the facts and do something about them or continue sticking our heads in the sand until the situation runs its course and time runs out.

Many times, when we finally do recognize the problem, we often respond in anger, which is usually directed at God. We blame Him for the situation we are in. After all, He is the Supreme Being, the all-knowing, and the all-powerful. He could have prevented our hardship. This anger represents the third stage I mentioned, and it usually ushers us straight into the fourth stage, where we ask, "Why me, Lord?"

These two particular stages—blaming God and asking "Why me?"—happen almost simultaneously. It is as though we have concluded that it's definitely His fault, but we are confused as to why He allows us to suffer. We hear about human trauma, tragedy, and illness all the time. We're fed a steady diet of it in the newspaper, on television, and on the radio. Our consciousness becomes seared. We become immune to tragedy—until it visits *us,* and we are the ones being talked about in hushed voices. All of a sudden, nothing seems to be in focus. With all the people in this universe that bad things could happen to, we really don't understand why this is happening to us.

We begin to ask questions like, "What have I done to deserve this?" or "Am I being punished for something?" We begin to justify our actions, our deeds, or our lifestyle to God, as though we need to convince Him that He made a mistake. From my personal experiences and from those of other cancer patients I know, visit, and consult with, I'm convinced that to get past this stage we have to come to an understanding of what cancer really is and what it is not. Eliminating some myths, along with some fears, is crucial.

I have read and studied about cancer extensively over the last twenty-three years. As I said, through my sphere of contacts and friends, I have received literally hundreds of books, tapes, herbs, and teas. Opinions, philosophies, and advice have been just as forthcoming. I've listened to all of it, and when you receive this much information, it can either serve for your good, or it can work against you! Here again, it's back to the question of choice.

Even though the abundance of information may sometimes confuse you, you are the one who determines which way to go.

CANCER: CAUSE AND EFFECT

What exactly causes cancer? We don't know everything for sure. But one thing is certain: there *are* things we can do to minimize our chances of getting cancer.

One important fact I learned is that we can greatly reduce our odds of having cancer by reducing the stress in our lives and by eating properly. There are a number of good books that address the value of good nutrition. All the articles and books on nutrition I have read indicate that we should eliminate the items I mentioned earlier: beef, pork, dairy products, refined white flour, sugar, caffeine, and salt.

Carl Simonton, in his book *Getting Well Again,* explains his theory that cancer is stress-related. Of the hundreds of patients he has treated over the years, without exception each has had an emotional crisis—the death of a loved one, the loss of a job, a divorce, or something of that nature—within an eighteen-month to two-year period before being diagnosed with cancer. How we respond emotionally to such crises can determine our outcome.

Another book I highly recommend is *Making Stress Work for You,* by Lloyd Ogilvy. The premise of this book is that we cannot live in a stress-free world, neither do we want to. The key is to learn that with God's help, we can make stress work for us and not against us. God is our Heavenly Father, and He wants only the best for us, His children. We find this principle confirmed in the Bible, in Matthew, Chapter 7. Even in our finite minds, we who are parents can understand that. If we want what's best for our children, how much more does our Heavenly Father want what is best for us?

Another book that helped enlighten me is *Recovery,* by Chuck Swindoll. He says that there are two types of sin: original and personal. Original sin can be traced back to Adam and Eve, the first humans, and their fall in the Garden of Eden. Their act of disobedience contaminated the entire human race, leaving all of mankind spiritually dead and distant from God (Romans 5:12). Personal sin, on the other hand, is an individual matter. We are sinful by nature because of the Fall, but when it comes to all the particular things we do wrong, we are sinners by choice, and our wrongdoing constitutes our personal sin. Original sin introduced sickness, suffering, and death into the human race, and all mankind suffers the consequences. But in addition, there often exists a direct relationship between personal sin and physical sickness.

There are numerous examples in Scripture of someone becoming ill because of personal sin. When King David sinned against God in his adulterous affair with Bathsheba, their first son died. Fortunately, in cases where sin is a problem, confession of sin is the first step toward healing. Sometimes, however, there is no relation between personal sin and physical sickness. One's illness cannot always be traced back to an act of disobedience. In John 9, for instance, we read about a man born blind not because of anyone's sin, but, rather, that God might be glorified.

In most instances, however, cancer is in some sense the result of violating the laws of nature. God has set laws into effect, and whenever anyone violates them, he or she must suffer the consequences. Now you may say, "What do you mean, 'violating the laws of nature'?" Well, let's start with some examples.

We all know what good nutrition is, yet we eat poorly and then wonder why we feel sluggish or get fat! We know that living stressfully is not good for our health, yet we live under excessive stress and often suffer the consequences. If, indeed, cancer results from improper nutrition and stress, it should not be hard to devise a plan to correct the situation. People who live in the West have poorer diets and live under greater stress than any of our counterparts around the world. It should be noted that we also have the greatest rates of not only cancer, but also heart failure, ulcers, and high blood pressure.

Although I believe that God doesn't cause cancer or want us to be sick, still these things serve a purpose. I cannot find, either in Scripture or in secular history, a person used greatly by God who did not have to suffer along the way. Just remember, it's not what happens to us that matters, it's what we do with it that counts.

What we have to do, if we want to see anything good come from it, is accept what happens to us. Before we can reach this stage, we must get our heads on straight. Until then, it's no good making decisions about what to do. Unless you have done your homework to help you understand the nature of the disease, you won't know how many of your fears are unnecessary. And as long as you are acting in fear, your decisions may be unhealthy. Reading Scripture is a powerful way to overcome fear.

Increasing our knowledge and strengthening our faith helps us move into the stage of acceptance. In acceptance, there is a tremendous burden lifted. It's as though we've come full circle. Yes, we're still scared, but we've begun to realize the importance of keeping the entire battle in perspective. We learn how to fight with every fiber of our bodies and, at the same time, avoid becoming full-time warriors. As an end in itself, battling cancer is not much of a life; there has to be time for God, family, and friends as well.

STEPS TO OVERCOMING FEAR

There are three things you have to do to overcome fear: you

have to identify your fears, you have to educate yourself about what you fear, and you then have to take action to overcome that fear.

First, it's important to identify exactly what you fear. You can't fight an enemy if you don't know what that enemy looks like. When you identify your fear, you are able to give it limits and deal with it so it's not so overwhelming.

Next, educate yourself. Find someone who has had the same fears that you have and discover what they did to overcome them. Awareness is a very important part of understanding anything in life. I know that with my cancer struggles, the more I could learn about the disease and the treatment of the disease, the better I could deal with it. The old saying, "Ignorance is Bliss" is very often *not* true. It's an exception to the rule, not the rule.

Finally, to overcome fear, you must take action. Facing what you fear and then acting upon it is the only way to get past it. Sometimes the things we fear are intangible. Yet, when you actually face your fear, you often find that the fear in your mind was far greater than reality.

CHAPTER 4

Day-by-Day Faith

At the end of my treatment in 1986, my tests said there were no active cancer cells in my body. My doctor announced that I was in complete remission. As I share this with you, it's important for you to understand that until 1986, even though I had a tremendous faith in God, I had never prayed for healing. I prayed for understanding, and I asked for help to be strong. I wanted to keep being brave because I knew "the heroes of this world are no braver than ordinary men, they're just brave five minutes longer."

The fact is that some of us are not healed in this life. We see specific cases in the Bible where godly, dedicated, spiritually pure men were subject to disease and weakness: Epaphroditus in Philippians 2, Trophimus in II Timothy 4, and, of course, the Apostle Paul with his thorn in the flesh. Even though it was not God's will that he be healed, Paul learned many valuable lessons as a result of his pain and affliction. Though Paul asked God to heal him three times, with sincere faith in God's ability to heal, God chose instead to use Paul's suffering to make him a better man. However, I believe many people are not healed simply because they do not ask God. In my case, once I finally did pray to be healed, God answered my prayer.

Please understand, I'm not saying my healing was instantaneous. Like most healing, mine took time. God used doctors, medical science and my own efforts to bring about my remission. We can help ourselves by using others' affirmations, by our own "self talk" and by surrounding ourselves with positive and upbeat people. We have to incorporate good nutrition, a positive attitude and self-control, both physical and mental. If these factors have not characterized our lives up to this point, then they have to be learned.

THE HEALING VISION

It has often been said that seeing is believing. Well, conversely, part of believing is seeing. I am speaking of "seeing" in your imagination, or visualizing. Visualization is important, especially in the treatment of cancer. In your mind, you see the cancer cells as the enemy and then imagine healthy cells destroying them. Some people visualize something akin to the electronic game PacMan, where the little, speeding PacMan comes in and gobbles up the cancer cells. Others imagine the malignant cells are grapes being plucked off the vine one by one until they are all gone. Still others pretend the tumor is a head of cauliflower: they break it off a piece at a time until it is totally eliminated. Many cancer research centers use this technique today with adults as well as with children.

But healing comes in many ways. The most powerful physical component of my healing was no doubt chemotherapy. Just like in visualization, chemotherapy is comprised of potent chemicals designed to seek out and kill cancer cells. Yet, in the process of killing the bad cancer cells, there are side effects that vary with the different chemicals used. Nobody can imagine the destructive way it works or the instant depression it can cause unless he has taken it himself. But again, recording my thoughts regularly on the good days played a big part in helping me keep my head above water.

On days when the chemo would get to me, when the depression was on the surface, I would go back and read of my blessings and determination written on my good days, and it would renew my strength. It helped me keep my spirits high.

Naturally, some types of chemotherapy have more severe side effects than others. The first one I was administered was Adromiacin, better known as "The Red Devil"—and believe me, it was a toughie. Remember, I flew down to Houston and back in one day because I wanted to be in my own home and in my own bed before I started throwing up! Anybody who's ever been sick away from home can appreciate the fact that when you're sick, you want to be in your own bed. That old saying, "There's no place like home," takes on new meaning!

You see, I didn't want people's sympathy—I didn't want

pity, I only wanted support from those who meant the most to me. I wanted understanding from my family and from my friends. As cancer patients, we just want to live as normal a life as possible and be treated with respect and dignity. We don't want to appear different or be treated as though we are.

How do you hang in there when it gets most difficult? Learning to adjust and be flexible in any situation is one of the most important lessons to be learned in life. For instance, in my treatment, the pump and the catheter I had to wear (satchel and all) were just plain ugly! Because of its bulk, it limited the style of clothing I could wear. However, my ability to make the most out of every situation saved the day! I never limited myself to wearing frumpy, baggy clothes. In fact, I still wore my halter tops and strapless dresses. I simply pinned a dumb old flower to the bandage and made it look as if it belonged there. If that didn't work, I put on a scarf, making sure it was strategically placed and looking like the latest fashion out of *Vogue!*

I knew that my creativity sprung from a motivation to fit in and look normal. I wanted to look and feel pretty in spite of everything. The lesson to be learned from this is that it is very important for each of us to do whatever it takes to help us feel our best—you and I know that keeping a healthy self-image is a constant challenge in the best of circumstances. Anything we can do to feel better about ourselves is certainly worth the time, the effort and the expense. And when it gets really tough, we must remember that God has promised us that He will never give us more than we can handle.

Those words sustained me on many occasions. One of the most challenging side effects of the chemotherapy for me was the loss of energy. Believe me, the fatigue that comes with chemotherapy is not like normal energy loss. It is extreme, and if you are normally a very energetic person, you have to fight hard not to become depressed over your inability to keep up the pace you want. It can be very frustrating.

In our fast-paced society, many people could stand to learn that it is okay to rest. It's good to lie down, it's not wrong to say "I don't feel well," and it's okay to sleep in late if you need to. Instead of feeling that these were signs of weakness or that I was a lesser person, I had to learn that it was really fine. I had to overcome the fear that I wasn't being an example of the courage that everyone expected me to have during this adversity.

I learned to make wise choices. If I wanted to attend one of my kid's ball games in the evening, then I needed to take a nap in the afternoon. I had to learn to leave the floors unmopped so I'd have the strength and energy to go to the game. That was okay. The secret is to get your priorities straight, set a reasonable pace, and *don't be too hard on yourself!*

It's easy for women to be hard on themselves, especially when it comes to weight. One of the more insidious side effects of the chemotherapy is weight fluctuation. For some it's a gain and for others, a loss. Why it seems to go only in the direction we don't want it to is beyond me! If being overweight has always been a problem, you'll probably gain, and if you've always been thin, you'll get thinner. It's really not fair, but, as we've already discussed, life isn't fair. I guarantee you one thing: it sure beats the alternative!

Another major concern that cancer patients have is relating well to their spouses. From years of social work and working in direct sales with people, I'm convinced that the strength of a relationship is determined long before cancer sets in. If two people keep the doors of communication open and know each other's wants and needs, then physical changes in the body are unimportant. If the physical changes do become overly important to the other person, remember, it is their problem. We can't take on that responsibility or that guilt. They may even need professional help. True masculinity or femininity is not determined by the body or by physical beauty but, rather, by an attitude. It's the heart that counts!

How you and I deal with situations will, for the most part, determine how our family responds. We know they love us. Their biggest challenge is knowing how to treat us. Oftentimes they don't know whether to hold us, hug us, cry with us, or to tell us a joke and make us laugh. Here again, their ability to cope will be determined by the relationship established prior to adversity. When you retain a normal lifestyle, when you maintain your sense of humor and are able laugh at yourself, when you are honest and up-front with your family about the facts and yet at the same time keep the entire situation in perspective, your family will adapt with little difficulty. I worked hard at keeping my family's lifestyle as normal as possible. It was just an accepted fact—I had cancer, and we could live with that.

Probably the most common struggle of all is that sometimes you just get tired of keeping up the fight. During my fifth year of chemotherapy, I would rather have been beaten with a stick than voluntarily take chemotherapy, knowing I would be sick again. I knew that food would lose its taste, smells and odors would cause sudden, violent reactions, and that nausea would be a full-time condition that no other person could help me bear. I knew I would constantly have hot flashes and my mouth would become so sore that I couldn't talk or eat for days at a time. You just get to the point where you wonder if the cure is worth the fight.

Well, trust me when I say, "Yes, it is!"

The secret is to take it minute by minute, hour by hour. Rely heavily upon your personal strength, the strength of your family, and above all the power of the Lord, and *you can make it!*

CHAPTER 5

Living, Laughing, and Loving

Often people come up and ask, "Rena, what's the most valuable lesson you've learned in all that you've been through?" The first thing that comes to my mind is how we need to live with a greater sense of *urgency!*

It breaks my heart when I see so many people just slither through life. They act as though they're going to live forever. Life is so short even at its best! Knowing each day is a precious gift motivates me to walk fast, talk fast, play fast, and work fast. There is so much I want to do, to see, to have, and to be. I know I'll never get through, but that's okay! I want to accomplish all I can in whatever length of time I have. Remembering that I have only so many years on this planet inspires me not to waste time. Once the moment is gone, you can *never* get it back again.

I've also learned to see the blessings in every situation.

You know, God's greatest gift to us is life, and what we do with our life is our gift back to Him. It's important to learn to see the blessings in the little things in life as well as in the big things.

For example, one fall I was on a business trip in New York City. Since I'm normally a very trusting person, I didn't give much thought to the risks of being in the "big city." I never dreamed that on my way home from the theatre, I would be mugged! The robbers literally ripped the jewelry from around my neck. It was over in a flash. They didn't harm me; they just grabbed my jewels and ran.

Some of my favorite Mary Kay jewelry was now high-tailing it down Madison Avenue! I really was very fond of my jewelry and what it represented, but rather than waste time bemoaning the loss of my precious jewelry, I thanked God that I was alive.

I always try to apply that same principle to the minor situations in life. Changing your thinking about little irritations can save a lot of frustration!

Over the years, I've learned to be more compassionate, more understanding, more patient with others, to be more aware of my own needs, and to live each day to the fullest. *None of us knows what tomorrow holds, but we do know Who holds tomorrow.*

I've always had a great desire to do things for the people I love, and during my cancer battle this proved to be a special blessing. I put the bulk of my time and energy into meeting other people's needs rather than worrying about my own problems. At the same time, I learned that asking for help is not a sign of weakness, as I once believed it was.

You see, there is a good reason things come in pairs. Highway patrolmen usually travel in pairs, foxholes are dug for two, and rarely is a ball game won without substitutions. I discovered that asking for help is okay! Everyone has problems, but every problem has a limited life span and usually holds positive possibilities. Every problem will change you, but it's up to you whether the change is for good or for bad.

Humor is one of the most important ingredients in my life. When we learn to laugh at ourselves, we'll never run out of something to laugh at. *We don't quit laughing when we grow old, we grow old when we quit laughing!* The value of life lies not in the number of its days but in what we make of each one. Man may live long yet get little from life. Whether or not you find satisfaction in life depends not on your number of years, but on your will.

It's never easy to keep reaching for dreams. When we realize non-demanding, easy accomplishments are seldom truly fulfilling, we don't need to try to take the easy way out or wait for success to come to us. Strength and courage can sometimes be lonely friends. *But those who continue to reach walk in stardust.* We're successful when we live life well, laugh often and love a lot. And with so many people to love and so many things to laugh at, we can't afford to live as if a single minute can be wasted.

Successful people fill their niche and accomplish their

task, leaving the world better than they found it. They realize true happiness comes from within and does not depend upon outward circumstances. Be committed to succeeding in your battle, whether it's against cancer or against your biggest fears. Keep your faith strong, your spirits high, and your determination unyielding.

TAKING RESPONSIBILITY
FOR YOURSELF

I have several pet peeves, and one of the greatest is people who never grow up and accept responsibility for their lives. Some folks are always blaming somebody or something for why they aren't where they ought to be. It's never their fault. Teenagers have a real challenge with that, don't they? Have you noticed that with many teens, fault lies always with their parents, teachers, cops, friends, and professors, but it never lies with them? Unfortunately, I know a number of adults who are that way as well! It's always somebody else's fault. They think it's the economy's fault, the government's, the neighborhood's, or the town's—they are always blaming somebody. It's time to grow up! You are responsible for *you*. To move forward, you have to accept responsibility and quit indulging in the follies of the past.

Understand: you can't change the past. No matter what has happened to you, good or bad, you can't change it. If you were beaten, if you were molested, abandoned, or whatever, you can't change it. The past is the past.

I remember one time I was talking to a group of women about achieving success. One of them came up to me and said, "Rena, you just don't understand how hard my life's been and all the things that have happened to me." She was right. I didn't understand her life. But what I told her was this: although we can't do anything to change the past, we can create the future.

I learned how powerful this concept was while I was talking to an elderly lady who had been abducted in her younger years. She had been raped, beaten, blinded, and mutilated and by God's grace, she lived to tell about it. She was remarkable. Someone once said to her, "You must have a horrible bitterness and resentment toward the man who did that to you." I'll never forget her response as it touched me deep, down inside. She said, "No, I'm not bitter. He had one night of my life. *He will never have another minute.*"

It takes a big person to be that mature. But we all have to *become* big people. We have to rise above the pettiness of others. It will always be out there. You see, there are plenty of insecure people in this world who have not learned that *blowing someone else's candle out does not make theirs any brighter.* It's sad but true. It's insecurity on the part of the individual.

I truly believe in teaching people the principles behind responsible action. We don't have time to sit down and talk to someone about every situation. That's why you learn the principle: you can take it home and apply it at any time. As the old adage says, "Give a man a fish, and he'll eat for a day. Teach a man to fish, and he'll eat for life."

This principle is the same one I reared my children on. I always taught my kids that if someone was ugly to them, whether in word or deed, and they responded in an ugly manner, they were no better than the other person was. They had to be the bigger person and rise above petty meanness.

Each of us has a "tape recorder" between his or her ears —a personal tape recorder that no one else can control. Instead of going back and replaying negative things—and we've all had the chance to record them—replay the good ones, the positive ones, the ones that uplift instead of degrade.

The key is to learn from the past, keep the lesson, and throw the experience away.

I hope I'm never put to the test on this one, but I truly believe that there isn't anything that could happen to me that I could not rise above. Does that mean I'm cold hearted and emotionless? Certainly not. I know I would go through a period of grieving if I lost a child, my husband, or my parents. What I am saying is that I refuse to let anything stop me from being the best I can be. And just as we can't afford to let other people's negativity bring us down, we also have to make sure that we don't discourage others.

One thing that has been helpful to me over the years is learning the art of being both honest and tactful at the same time. Those two things are linked together like a chain. Honesty is important. Yet, being sensitive and tactful is as important as being honest. It grieves me to see people "telling the truth" but being really hurtful in what they say and how they say it.

A good rule of thumb is not only to ask yourself "Is it true?" but also "Is it helpful? Does it build up or does it tear down?" If the answer is "it's going to tear down," I don't care how true it is, don't say it!

For the most part, we women don't take criticism very well. So when we have to deliver criticism (and those in positions of leadership sometimes have to), there is a tendency to try and sandwich it between a whole lot of praise. Two thick, thick layers of praise and a little thin layer of criticism. Actually, I don't even like the word "criticism" as much as I do "suggestions." Since many of us have been hurt in the past, we immediately get defensive. That is human nature. My immediate reaction when someone starts telling me that I'm doing something wrong is, "I am not!"

It's very, very difficult for any of us to be objective about ourselves. We can see someone else's faults so much more easily than we can see our own. Often the things we pick out as faults in others are the very things we ourselves are weak in, so we have to learn to be tactful and humble. Never be too big to say, "I'm wrong," "I made a mistake," or "I'm sorry." Part of being responsible is admitting our mistakes.

This leads to what I think is the key ingredient in effectively working with other people: good communication skills. So many times, what is heard is not what you said, and sometimes what you said is not what you mean. Suddenly, there's a problem!

One of the most essential elements of good communi-cation skills is simply to be a good listener. In fact, listening is a skill. You can *learn* to listen.

I've always liked the saying, "God gave us two ears and one mouth so we can listen more than we talk." One way you can make sure you are listening is by simply repeating the question. "Nancy, let me make sure I understand what you're saying. I think you said such and such... Am I correct?" I need to make sure I understand what she said and that what she said is what she meant.

Communication is not just audible; it's also visible. There's so much that we convey non-verbally. For instance, with a simple roll of the eyes, you don't have to say another word; I'll get the message. Folding your arms across your chest will shut people out. It may be a habit you didn't realize you had; but if you have it, work at breaking it! It says to people that you really don't want to listen to what they have to say. There are a lot of little habits that keep us from becoming good communicators, and it is our responsibility to correct them. But remember the most important step towards being better communicators is simple: listen more than you talk!

CHAPTER 6

Getting Down to Business

It seems like it was back in the dinosaur ages when I was first introduced to Mary Kay Cosmetics. It was 1967, and I was a young mother living in government housing. Yes, you read it right: government housing. As I said before, Eddie was a social worker and didn't make a whole lot of money, so we lived in housing that was subsidized. But not having a lot of money wasn't unusual for either one of us.

I grew up poor materially—rich in love—but poor materially! I realized at a very young age that I could never compete with other kids materially; I would never have the new cars or pretty clothes. I knew there was one area I could compete in and always win hands down, however: I could be the best friend you've ever had!

When my "people skills" first began to bloom, I became one of the most popular girls in high school: I was class president, drill team captain, and head of just about anything else I was involved in. I loved every minute of high school!

Although it may sound strange to some today, I had absolutely no aspirations to go on to college. Even though I graduated third in my class of several hundred, I turned down all the college scholarships I was offered. I decided early on what I wanted to be—a loving, Christian wife and mother.

When I was seventeen years old I met and married Eddie Tarbet. Eddie had just graduated from college with a degree in Bible. He was a wonderful man who, like me, had grown up very, very poor. After we married, we continued to live in the "lifestyle to which we were accustomed"—a lifestyle of being *very* poor materially! We soon had three beautiful children and, although we were broke, we were as happy as could be!

Eddie received an offer for a new job, and we picked up our little family and moved from outside San Antonio to the big city of Ft. Worth, Texas. When we arrived, I only knew one person in the entire Dallas/Ft.Worth area. That one friend, Jana Cox, had become a part of "Mary Kay Cosmetics,"—whatever that was!

I was a full-time, stay-at-home mom with three little kids living in a two-bedroom apartment. It would be safe to say my wardrobe was far from glamorous! In fact, I didn't even wear make-up (when I was growing up only "fast" girls wore makeup!). I was lucky if I got to take a quick shower; good skin care was not a part of my routine.

I vividly remember the day Jana called and said she wanted to share a product with me. She proceeded to introduce me to the "basic skin care set" which back then cost $15.95 and was an enormous amount of money to me. Jana knew our financial situation, so she let me purchase the basic set at wholesale and put it on layaway. (This is unheard of today. In fact, one of the first things we teach a new consultant is that you don't let your best friend or even your *mama* have it wholesale!) For the next four weeks I scrimped and saved my household money until I finally paid off my basic skin care set. Not long after that, Jana called and invited me to go to a meeting with her, a Mary Kay sales meeting.

Let me paint you a picture here. I stayed home by choice. I didn't want my kids in a day care center. I wanted to raise my own kids and make all the mistakes myself! I was happy. I had a wonderful husband and three beautiful babies. I was doing what I had chosen to do.

Still, there was a void, an emptiness that was deep down, and I have to admit I was going a little nutty. When you have a five-year-old, a three-year-old, and a one-year-old, and you don't have a car, money, or friends, it's not hard to wonder whether you'll end up in a room with padded walls!

Even though I had great kids, they were still kids. Anywhere I went in the house, the battle cries would sound: "Help, let me in, he hit me, he cheated, he touched me, he looked at me, it's my turn!"

A friend of mine said that one day she had her kids in the car, and her daughter yelled, "Mommy, tell him to stop it." The mom asked what her brother was doing that was so irritating, and the little girl said, "He's looking out my window!"

So along comes Jana, and she says, "Rena, come to a meeting with me. I'd love to buy you dinner, and I'll even be happy to pay your babysitter." Those words were music to my ears. I couldn't have cared less where we were going! I didn't go to the meeting to check out "a better way of life," or because I was looking for a part-time job. I went for a free dinner, free babysitting, and a welcome night away from home! Yet attending this Mary Kay meeting had to be one of the most significant experiences in my life.

Let me set the stage so you'll understand why.

As I said, I was living in government housing on $300 a month and $10 a week for groceries (those were the days!). Things that you and I take for granted today, I never had when I was growing up. I had never owned Kleenex in my life, and I never had paper towels or aluminum foil. We had concrete floors, and scorpions would actually crawl up my legs! (Yes, scorpions are indigenous to the southwest!) My babies grew up with powdered milk in their bottles since whole milk wasn't an option.

Don't get me wrong, I'm not complaining; since you can't miss what you don't know about. At the time, my life was exactly what I expected it to be. But you can imagine how awkward I felt when I heard this group of women talking about diamonds, mink coats, dream vacations, and pink Cadillacs. I felt like a duck out of water!

Mary Kay Cosmetics, Inc., was only four years old at the

time. One of the principles Mary Kay integrated into her new company (which she founded after she retired and her children were grown, by the way) was the importance of recognition. She wanted women to win awards that were both pretty and useful—but more important, she wanted women to compete against themselves, *not* against other people.

At the meeting that night, although I couldn't relate to what these women were talking about, I was very impressed with the ladies themselves. They had a spirit about them that I'll never forget. They were warm, friendly, and they were excited! Moreover, I couldn't believe how encouraging they were to each other.

That particular night the topic of discussion was goal setting. They asked the question, "Where are you going to be in five years?" I remember sitting there thinking to myself, "I'll probably be exactly where I am now, only the kids will be five years older."

As the meeting progressed, I realized that I wasn't using all of my God-given talents. I knew I was capable of doing more than scrubbing floors and washing diapers—although I'm not putting that down. There is no more noble profession in the world than that of wife and mother! But I realized I could do that and more, and do it all well.

Having no idea what I was getting into, I signed my agreement to become an independent beauty consultant. I just knew I wanted something these women had.

Looking back, I have to admit that the odds were against

me. I didn't have a car, I didn't have any money, I didn't know anybody, and I didn't wear any make-up. Not only that, I had a husband who didn't want me working outside the home, and I didn't want a career!

Yet I soon discovered that inside of me, there was a little eaglet waiting to soar. I wanted a better way of life, and I was willing to put forth the effort. Thus, my lifelong adventure in Mary Kay began.

It has been a long journey. I wasn't an overnight success. And faced with the choice, I would rather describe myself as a rising star than a shooting star. A big key to my success has been that I have always worked consistently, competing only with myself. My goal is always to be better this year than I was last year. It's been a layering effect. I didn't build my business as quickly as many do today. (Of course, we didn't have the training or tools that are available today, either!) There wasn't a "career path" to hop onto.

Actually, we were the pioneers blazing the trail, trying to figure out what worked and what didn't. We did it by trial and error. I was determined to learn and grow from every experience, especially those that did not turn out the way I wanted them to. I held twenty skin care classes before I had a $100 class and then another forty-eight before I had the next $100 class. I was discouraged and frustrated, but it never crossed my mind to quit. I had made a commitment to myself the day I signed my agreement that I would not quit until I was a pro, and it was evident I wasn't one yet!

I think the most accurate way to describe my journey is with the words "plug, plug, plug." Consistent effort paid off. I was Queen of my unit for three consecutive years before I became a Sales Director—not because I was very polished, but because I consistently put in the effort. Expending the effort necessary to be successful is a process I truly enjoy. I have always been very self-disciplined, a trait that I've discovered is a rarity. I know what I want from life, I know what it takes to get it, and I am willing to pay the price, or as I prefer to phrase it— *enjoy* the price!

GETTING TO KNOW YOURSELF

I'm continually amazed at the large number of people who have no earthly idea what they want from life. They can name their three favorite television programs, who stars in them, and exactly what time they come on. But they couldn't name their three major goals in life if their lives depended on it.

People ask me all the time, "What keeps you going, Tarbet?"

There are a number of things that keep me going. One of the biggest things is achieving my goals. Setting goals involves knowing what you want, when you want it, and what you have to do to get it. It is truly that simple! And I am one of the most goal-oriented people you will ever know.

The late H.L. Hunt (who before his death was one of the richest men in the world) was a guest on a television show a number of years ago. One of the commentators asked him, "What is the secret to your success?" I happened to be walking through a room when I heard the question put to him. I ran like lightening to get my tape recorder. I wanted to record these profound words of wisdom. Mr. Hunt stood up and said, "Decide what you want from life, decide what price you're willing to pay, and then be about your work." Then he sat down.

I was, quite frankly, a little disappointed his words weren't more profound. But as I reflected on them that day, I realized he was absolutely right. It really is that simple. Thirty years later, I understand them even better than I did then!

Just answer these two questions: What do you want from this life? What price are you willing to pay? Then *get busy and go to work!* That is what getting to know yourself is all about.

Many folks just go through the motions of living. You know them, and I know them. They get up every morning, go to their jobs and moan, groan, gripe and complain. They come home at night, eat dinner, become a couch potato, go to sleep, then get up and do it all over again. They can't wait for the weekend to utter those sweet words, "Thank God it's Friday." They live for their two-week vacation—two short weeks out of fifty-two. What a miserable existence!

This isn't the kind of life most people want.

Unfortunately, it's easy to know what you don't want, but it's agonizingly hard for most people to define what they *do* want. If I said, "List your five greatest faults," most people would find it an easy task. They could whip them out quickly. We can all tear ourselves down without difficulty, but if I said "list your five greatest assets," you would probably get your first two or three, and then you'd stop and be uncertain as to what to put next.

Another question to ask yourself might be, "If money was no object and you were guaranteed you couldn't fail, how would you be living?" For example, where would you want to live: the city, the country or a farm perhaps? What kind of car would you drive? How would you dress? Would you go to Europe three or four times a year? Would you have a personal masseuse that came to your house? Would you have fresh flowers delivered every day? Would you have a yardman, a housekeeper or a "go-fer?"

What is it that you want from life? If God gives you another ten years to live, twenty years to live, or fifty years to live, what are you going to do with it? What price are you paying for the space you occupy on this earth? What are you doing to leave this world a better place than you found it?

Get out a sheet of paper and write down what you want. Then simply believe wholeheartedly that if you have the ability to think it and dream it, you have the God-given ability to *achieve it!* God won't give us a dream bigger than the wherewithal He gives us to accomplish it.

CHAPTER 7

Keys to Success

Besides having a humble heart and spirit, I've discovered various "keys"—specific things, ideas, and strategies—that will help you become successful or more successful in whatever you endeavor.

First, you have to understand that habits of success or failure are learned. We aren't born consistent, and we're not born self-disciplined. But we aren't born procrastinators either!

Consistency and self-discipline are things that are *learned.* I've always loved the song in the old Rogers and Hammerstein musical *South Pacific* that says we are taught to love and hate. We intuitively know that prejudices and hatred are learned— and, if that is true, it stands to reason we can unlearn them, or re-condition ourselves.

A special key is *desire.* Pay close attention here because I think this is one of those simple secrets all very successful people know... and knowing this can make all the difference in your life: when it comes to success, you have to *want* to be successful.

Now you may be saying to yourself, "That's nothing remarkable, Rena. Everybody wants to be successful." Well, I used to think that was true, but it's not. I'm truly amazed by the number of people who deep down and at the gut-level do *not* want more out of life. I think we've been conditioned by our culture to believe it's okay to be average. My friends, *average* is not a good word!

Do you know that when you're average, you are as close to the bottom as you are to the top? Think about it a moment. If that is true, there isn't much pride in being average! Remember what average means... you take the highest score (say 100) and the lowest score (say 0) and divide by two to get the average: fifty—right smack in the middle. So average isn't necessarily very good at all.

Many people today look at everybody else and say, "Well, at least I'm doing better than so-and-so over there." That kind of thinking is the reason the bulk of America today is average.

The hardest part in getting to the top is getting through the crowd at the bottom! You see, most people aren't at the top—in fact, the masses are at the bottom. The higher up the pinnacle you go, the less competition you face. If it's lonely at the top, you can be sure it's not lonely at the bottom! Being on the bottom can be bittersweet comfort: when you're on the bottom you don't have to feel you're the only one there. There are a whole bunch of people just like you! You can even justify where you are and why you should stay there. But you'll never become truly successful by being content sitting at the bottom.

Success is something you've got to want so badly that you'll do whatever is necessary to get there, as long as it is honest, legal, and morally right.

Now, I don't presume to know what success means for you. Success means different things to different people.

Success is not necessarily measured by how big a house you have, how much money you've made or what your tax return says. Success is persevering in the quest for goals. It costs no more to dream a big dream than to dream a little dream. My favorite definition of success is, "Getting out of life what you want, when you want it, without stepping on someone else to do it."

Did you know that there is a difference between desire and *burning* desire? It's not just a small difference—it's a huge difference. I define it this way: Burning desire is the "want-to" after the excitement's gone. Most of us, when we first start working toward a goal, have desire. But before we can reach that goal, desire has to become burning desire, or we'll never persevere and achieve that goal.

Have you ever noticed how excitement fades? We go to a seminar, a workshop, or a revival meeting, and we get all revved up. Outside stimuli are quite powerful. And for most people, it's easy to get revved up. It's *staying* revved up that is the tough part!

Is it easy for me? Absolutely not! Like everybody else, I

sometimes don't feel like working. But I work anyway because I want the results that will come from the effort. You can't run on emotions alone—emotions lie to you. That is why you must have a burning desire to be successful regardless of how you feel.

On top of that, to become successful you also have to be dissatisfied with where you are. People sometimes take the word "dissatisfied" to mean "unhappy." However, you can be very happy and still be dissatisfied.

Remember, when I first went to work as a young mother, I had a wonderful husband and three precious little ones. Being a full-time mom was exactly what I'd wanted to do since I was twelve years old. I wanted to be married to a good man and be a good Christian wife and mother. That is exactly what I was doing, and I was truly happy.

Yet deep down inside, there was a void in my life, an emptiness I couldn't put my finger on. Not that what I was doing wasn't good. I was simply becoming aware of a need to be more than just a good wife and mom. I realized I was dissatisfied and wanted more out of life—primarily for my kids and Eddie. That dissatisfaction motivated me to change.

Dissatisfaction motivates us to make all kinds of changes. Take dieting, for instance (the vast majority of women can relate to anything about dieting!). I can stand here and tell you how I hate my body and want to lose twenty pounds, and I can truly mean it. It's not lip service—I have a sincere, genuine desire. But offer me some pizza in a few hours and see what I do. You'd think I'd never seen food in my life!

In the face of temptation, good old-fashioned desire just isn't enough to sustain you through the tough times. It's easy to say "I want this" or "I want that," but do you want it badly enough to develop the daily self-discipline to obtain it?

Until a person is dissatisfied with where they are, they won't step out of their comfort zone. It's only when we're stretched outside of our comfort zone that we grow. As long as we stay content in our comfort zone, not only are we not going to grow, we're going to become average.

There may be rare exceptions, but most people can only stay average for a limited amount of time. It's like treading water. Treading water is better than drowning, but you can only tread water for so long before you go under for the last time. You soon reach the point where you sink or swim!

This point is crucial to understand: Don't settle for less out of fear. Don't lower your sights because you're afraid you won't reach your goals. Don't refuse to commit yourself just because you think that if you don't make it then you'll have egg on your face. My friends, *dream big!* Set big goals! As I said, it costs no more to dream a big dream than it does to dream a little-bitty dream!

Some of us naturally think bigger than others. But, no matter what, if you can think it, you can achieve it. That is what's so exciting to me. People ask me all the time, "You keep us going, Rena, but what keeps *you* going?" I have all kinds of personal support, but as I said earlier, it is mainly my goals that keep me going. If they weren't so big, they wouldn't motivate me so.

Is it easy? No. When you are successful, there will always be people who will take pot shots at you and criticize you or worse, but you must continue to press on. Here's what gives me the strength to go on in the face of past hurts and disappointments:

First, I find great strength in the fact that Christ, who is the Son of God and perfect in every way, was criticized, talked about, and betrayed by everyone. Yet even though He was hurt and disappointed, He rose above it and continued toward His purpose. Since I know I'm far from being perfect, it's a great comfort to me to see how He loved even the hateful people He encountered and how He continued on in His purpose.

Second, I try to remember that when you're kicked in the rear, at least you know you're out front! Being out front is always risky. But unless you're the lead dog, the scenery never changes. In order to see the beauty, you have to be out front.

Is it possible to get beyond other people's pessimism and criticism and take the risk to move forward? Absolutely. There is always a way if we're willing to take the chance to find it out.

Now, my next point is not a very popular message. But it's necessary to say. Friends, it's time to quit blaming others for our station in life. I've got news for you: you are where you are because of the choices you've made, whether they were good or bad, wise or foolish, conscious or unconscious. The clothes you have on today, the house you live in, and the car you drive are all your choices. We base our choices on how we see ourselves. This is the main reason learning to see ourselves in a favorable light is so important. Increasing your self-esteem will make a tremendous difference in how you see yourself, how you look at circumstances, and how you make decisions.

Well-meaning friends may sometimes come along and try to discourage us. But you know what? Discouragement is the devil's number one tool. As one story has it, when they sold all the devil's tools in the auction, the tool of discouragement went for the highest price. You see, if the devil can get you and me discouraged, all the rest of his weapons will work automatically.

I am reminded of the story of the man who went to work, opened his lunch pail, and said to his buddy, "Yuck. Peanut butter sandwiches again. I am so sick and tired of peanut butter sandwiches—every day it's peanut butter sandwiches, and I'm sick of them." The man he was sitting with said, "Well, why don't you ask your wife to make you something different?" And the man said, "Oh, I'm not married—I make my own lunch!"

We're all going to have "peanut butter sandwiches" until we make something different for lunch.

Our culture reinforces negativity. If you grew up in an average home (not a "bad" home, but an average one), by the time you were eighteen years old you would have already been told a minimum of 147,000 times what you couldn't do. So is it surprising that seventy-seven percent of everything that falls out of your mouth is negative? Most of the time negativity is so much a part of us, we're not even aware of it.

We run around saying things like, "You know, I'm just no

good in math" or "I come by it naturally; my daddy isn't good in math" or "I can smell food and gain weight" or "Everything I eat turns automatically to fat" or "Just call me 'Grace'—I'll probably spill it." We run around all day long saying negative things and then wonder why we get negative results.

Can we get rid of negativity? You bet! But here's the catch: When we eliminate the negative, we have to replace it with the positive. If all you do is eliminate the negative and you don't replace it with positive, the negative will come back, just like a boomerang!

Remember, we live in a negative world, and none of us is going to change that. There are people out there right now just waiting to rain on your parade. Most of the time, they aren't even aware they are doing it. They are just "concerned" for you. They want you to know "why it won't work" and why you ought to "cut your losses" and why you should realize that "God's trying to tell you something."

We all have reasons to fail. We could sit here and talk about illness and death and job layoffs and financial stress and aging parents and teenagers with drug abuse and DWI's and kids with learning disabilities... the list could go on and on. Nobody's immune to the problems of the world. Everybody has problems. In fact, I *hope* you have problems, because the only people I know who don't have any problems are six feet under!

Let me give you my favorite definition of a problem: A problem is the space between where you are and where you want to be. Another way to put it is: a problem is something between what you already have and what you still want to achieve.

Every one of us should be in the problem-*solving* business. Have you ever noticed that whenever you bridge the gap between where you are to where you wanted to be, suddenly you want to be somewhere else? It's true for *all* of us. We bridge one gap and then up comes another one. We'll never be without problems. It's a fact of life, and it's okay! Accepting that life is full of problems is one of the first steps toward moving forward.

One of the most common phrases I hear people say is, "When I get my act together, I'll do such and such." It drives me crazy when I hear that because, unfortunately, none of us will ever get his act together completely. It's like saying, "I'm going to eat dinner once and for all." It just doesn't happen that way.

I've faced some big challenges in my life—I mean *big* challenges. I've come to realize that if you wait for the waters to be smooth before you set sail, you'll never lose sight of the shore. My friends, we can learn to sail only when the wind is blowing, and that means we'll probably be on choppy waters.

That is a very important point. Life is a sea of choppy waters, a continual series of crises of one kind or another. Just about the time we get one thing fixed, something else comes up. We get an issue sorted out and something else comes up. It's going to be that way all our lives.

Some people, because of their conditioning, always see the negative in every situation. They blow my mind! It doesn't matter what you say, they'll see the bad instead of the good.

It reminds me of a story about two farmers who lived next door to each other. One of them was an optimist and the other was a pessimist. One would always find something good to say, and the other would always find something bad. The optimistic farmer would say, "Look at that sunshine. Isn't God good? It's sure going to help our crops grow," and his neighbor would respond, "Yeah, and it'll probably just keep on until it burns up all our crops." Or the one farmer would say, "Isn't this rain wonderful? God is so good—He's given the corn a drink today," and the other would retort, "Yeah, it'll probably just keep on until it washes the seed right out of the ground. We won't even have a crop this season."

One day the optimist farmer decided he was going to teach his friend a lesson. So he went out and bought a bird dog, the best dog that money could buy, and he taught him tricks that no dog had ever done before. He worked and worked with the dog, and when he finally had him totally trained, he invited his friend to go duck hunting with him. They went out on a boat, and a duck flew over. They both shot at the duck, and the duck fell to the water. The positive farmer turned to his dog and said, "Go get 'em, boy." The dog jumped out of the boat and walked on the water! The optimist farmer thought to himself, "I've got him now—there is not a single negative thing he can say about that." He nudged his buddy and said, "What do you think about that?" The pessimistic farmer immediately replied, "Can't swim, can he?"

Some people are <u>determined</u> to see the negative. We just have to overlook those folks—we can try to help them, but we can't let them pull us down.

ATTITUDE

Attitude is such a difficult thing to define, isn't it? It's not a tangible thing. I guess the most amazing thing to me is that people who have a bad attitude seldom think they do. And yet attitude determines our actions and actions determine our "altitude," or how high we will go.

A positive attitude is something we have to work at every day of our life. It's not one of those things you can "set" and then you just sit back and relax. It doesn't work that way because as soon as you think your attitude is good, along comes somebody to rain on your parade again!

Take enthusiasm, for instance. When we first try to sell a product we love, we may not have all the fine details nailed down, but we can sell a ton of product on an enthusiastic attitude alone. Even if we do the wrong things, if our attitude is good, things can turn out okay.

On the other hand, we can do all the "right" things—recite a script written by the most successful sales person ever, memorized word for word, and delivered with precision—but if we have a rotten attitude, it just won't work.

We don't have to understand why or how attitude is so influential, but we need to believe it is—because it's true. Here is an illustration. I don't understand how the telephone transmits sound. I don't understand technically how you can pick up a phone in America and talk to someone in Germany—the sound waves traveling across the wire on the bottom of the ocean or in the air—and they hear you even as you speak. It is truly beyond my comprehension! Yet, it's not necessary for me to understand it to believe the telephone works and to enjoy its benefits.

It's the same way with attitude. I don't try to understand how it works, I just know what a profound difference it makes when a good attitude is at work. It may not be tangible, but your attitude shows in everything you do.

One of my favorite illustrations is from my good friend Zig Ziglar, who says, "A positive person is one who goes after Moby Dick in a row boat… and takes the tarter sauce with him!"

Let me give you some suggestions that anyone can use to help improve their attitude.

NUMBER 1:

ASSOCIATE WITH
POSITIVE PEOPLE

I remember my grandmother saying, "I'll tell you who you are by the company you keep." For the most part, since we are like the people we associate with, we have to choose our friends wisely. If they're negative people, don't just walk away from

Baby Rena!

Rena with her mom and dad, brother Donald, and sister Vera

Rena—the high school graduate!

Tennis star Rena (1960). She was selected as the most athletic in her high school.

Rena's engagement photograph (July 1960)

Rena with her children— Jeff, Brian and Kim.

Eddie, Rena, Jeff, Kim, and Brian (1969)

Rena and Eddie together at a Mary Kay seminar. Rena was named the #1 Director in personal sales for the entire nation!

*Rena and her
first pink
Cadillac
(1973)*

*The Tarbet family
in 1974.*

In 1976, Rena was recognized as one of Mary Kay's Top 10 in the nation— her first time to achieve such status.

Rena speaks to a Mary K crowd in 1983.

Rena and Mary Kay Ash together in 1980.

Rena and Eddie's home in Colleyville, Texas.

...ena with ...r parents ...ugust, 1997)

*Rena and
Eddie at a g
event in 199*

Rena with Mary Kay, September 199.

them—run away from them!

Just because people like some of the same things you do, it doesn't mean they're positive people. You may need to get away from some of your negative friends precisely because you have something in common with them—namely a bad attitude. You become like the people you associate with. That is a Biblical truth.

Choose people who are upbeat and who work toward being positive themselves. One of the reasons support groups like Weight Watchers are so popular is that they are made up of people who are committed to the same worthy goal. People who are dieting don't need to be spending a lot of time with thin friends who always want to get together to chat at Baskin Robbins! It's much easier to stay focused and positive when you're with people who understand you and support you.

NUMBER 2:

FEED YOUR MIND
EVERY DAY OF YOUR LIFE

We worry so much about feeding our bodies. But we need to be feeding our minds positive things because what we put in is what we get out. As they say of computers, "Garbage in, garbage out."

I could get on my soapbox and talk all day long about what horrible things we feed our minds. I get really upset about what we, as American adults, dump into our minds—from soap operas to trashy books and novels to magazines sold at the grocery store. Then we act shocked when trashy things come out of our minds and out of our mouths! What goes in our minds influences our whole lifestyle.

Study after study shows that TV has a profound influence on how we think and behave. One of the reasons the term "couch potato" resonates with us is that we understand that the person sitting around watching TV is mindless. He turns on the TV, turns off his brain and lives via his imagination the trash that's on the screen. What a waste!

We have a responsibility to feed our minds with good things. I get all riled up when people say it doesn't matter what we watch or read. They think they can defy their negative environment. It's impossible to put trash in your mind and not get trash out. They're defying God's Word. You reap what you sow; if you plant potatoes, you get potatoes. And when you plant a pea, you don't get back one pea: you get a bushel of peas. One negative thought produces a heap of negative thoughts, just as one positive thought leads to even more positive thoughts. You can't defy this principle.

Actually, why anyone would want to watch the trash on TV is beyond me. If television shows don't represent the way you want to live your life, then why would you want to watch someone else living that way?

The longer I live, the more I realize that the mind controls the body. My friends, your mind can make you sick, and your mind can make you well. Because of my fight with cancer, I've studied this subject, and what I've said is a proven fact. I've learned that lots of us who have no medical reason to be living—absolutely none—are alive simply because we have a burning desire to live. The will to live—the positive input, the grit, the fight, and the determination—keep us going. The mind can make us a failure, or it can make us a success.

NUMBER 3:

WHAT YOU THINK ABOUT, YOU BRING ABOUT

It follows from what I've said that you generally get what you expect. When you expect to do well, you do well. If you don't think you will, you won't. It's actually that simple! That doesn't mean we can just sit back and wait for things to happen, of course. I remember hearing a story about two little boys who missed the school bus. One of them sat down to pray about it, and the other one took off running for the bus. The boy who was sitting down to pray said to his friend, "You mean, you're not going to pray that God will help us?" The other boy turned around and said, "Yeah, I'm just going to pray while I run!"

I've never been, and never will be, the sort of person to fold my arms across my chest and say, "Well, you know, if God wanted me to be a millionaire, I would be a millionaire." Nothing happens unless you go out there and do your part. God's not going to miraculously make you a millionaire overnight. The odds of becoming a millionaire are much better if you work toward your goal than if you only try to win the lottery.

I've always loved the principle that "we should pray as if everything depends upon God and work as if everything depends on us." You may remember the story of the little sparrow in the Bible. The sparrow is considered to be the most insignificant of birds, and yet the Bible says, God knows the number of feathers on their bodies. God knows when even one of them falls to the ground. But even though God watches over them, they still have to go out and find their own worms. Just as in our lives, some days are better for the birds than others. When the rains come and the ground is lush, those little worms crawl up to the top and that birdie can simply swoop down, get his worm and go on his merry way. But when the times are tough, when the ground is dry and cracked from drought, that same little bird has to scratch and dig. The worms are there, but God doesn't just drop them in the bird's open mouth.

There's an important principle here. More likely than not, to get your reward, you'll have to get out there and scratch and dig. There are times when it takes more digging than others. For example, if the economy is down, and we are in sales, we know it will affect all of us in some measure. Well, if you know that going in, you prepare accordingly. Be ready to scratch harder. It's the tough times that make us who we are. If I'm booking appointments, I can count on having a high percentage of postponements and a high percentage of cancellations in a time where everybody is just trying to make ends meet. Those are the times I don't fight the system; I simply work accordingly.

NUMBER 4:
LEARN TO SEE THE GOOD IN EVERY SITUATION

Learning to see good is an acquired mindset. Anything we do on a regular basis becomes a habit, and attitude is no exception. Habits are hard to make, and they're hard to break (isn't it amazing, though, how it always seems harder to make the good ones and break the bad ones!).

For example, when I had my chemotherapy, I lost all of my hair on my body at least three different times. I'm not saying I didn't have down times or feel ugly. I did. But I learned to say to myself, "Well, at least I don't have to shave my legs or tweeze my eyebrows!"

Most of the time, it's the little things that get to us. Have you ever had one of those mornings when you're in a hurry and you start to pull on a brand new pair of pantyhose and you cram your finger through them? You've suddenly got a huge hole. When this happens to me, rather than get upset, I've trained myself to say, "Well, that's one pair I don't have to wash!" It's an automatic reflex because I've *trained* myself.

I'm always surprised to see that some people even let the weather control their emotions. How stupid! We have no control whatsoever over the weather, so why let it ruin your day? Or somebody might say some wimpy, dippy little thing, and we let it devastate us. As if someone else's opinion could matter that much!

Don't let somebody else control how you feel and how you act. Stay in control of your emotions by insisting on seeing good in all things.

I must warn you: you can learn patience and control only through trying circumstances—which means you have to think of each situation as practice for the next! So don't be too hard on yourself. Find little victories and work your way up. Look for opportunities to exhibit control and a positive attitude. It's my guess that those opportunities are right around the corner.

Keys That Will Open Hundreds of Doors

THE #1 KEY:

LEARN THE JOY OF HARD WORK

I believe, for the most part, that we've failed to teach our young people today the rewards of hard work and a job well done. Now, don't get me wrong. I'm not down on young people—I have three wonderful, grown children remember? It seems, however, that there are a growing number of people who aren't interested in working, let alone doing hard work.

This is another one of my hot buttons! As a result of my work in direct sales, and because of Eddie's job as a social worker, I'm aware of just how many people today don't want to work. Most people who are on welfare or collecting unemployment wouldn't go to work if you offered them a job on a silver platter—they have three more months of unemployment money coming, and they intend to get it!

In my grandparent's days, when folks parted company, they said, "Work hard." Then between the 1950s and the 1970s people said, "Don't work too hard!" And now in the 1990s we say, "Take it easy."

See how much we've changed? I don't think we even realize it!

I can remember my junior high school teacher Mrs. Nixon, who taught us the word "initiative." I can still see her writing on the board, "Initiative is doing more than is expected of you." What do most people try to do today? They try and see how *little* they can get by with.

My youngest son Brian once got a summer job with a bunch of his friends at the Dallas/Ft. Worth airport. The job wasn't particularly glamorous. The kids would go out on a truck at seven in the morning and be dropped off along the highway to pick up trash, weeds and debris. Then one day, Brian came home and told me his boss had said, "I don't care if you pull only one weed a day—you be sure you're pulling it when the big boss comes by." Brian quit that job, and I was glad. I don't want my son working for someone who teaches his workers to see how little they can get away with.

What ever happened to "eight hours work for eight hours pay" and thirteen eggs to the dozen? What ever happened to "going the extra mile"? If you're going to make it on your own in life, it takes hard work. If you plan to inherit money, on the other hand, or if you don't mind being mediocre all your life, certainly you can get by on just a little effort. But if you truly want to make it on your own, it takes hard work.

People sometimes ask me, "How many hours a week do you work, Rena?" I just want to giggle every time someone asks me that—for several reasons. I usually reply, "Well, let's define work. If you define when I'm in the hot tub, planning the calendar under the stars as work, I do quite a bit of work. If traveling with my good friends on business and sitting up late into the evening talking is work, then I work a lot! So it all depends on how you define 'work'."

I believe in the old saying, "If you love your work, you'll never *work* another day in your life." I love what I do. I work hard, but I enjoy it; in fact, I thrive on it. It fills my social needs, recognition needs, and financial needs. You couldn't drive me away from my work with a stick. So I forget to view what I do as work, for starters.

The second way I usually answer that question is by saying, "Let me ask you a question first. You're a mother. How many hours a day are you a mother?" We all know mothers are mothers 24 hours a day, 7 days a week, 365 days a year. "How many hours a week are you a Christian?" If you're a Christian, you're a Christian all day, every day.

Does that mean that you're involved in "motherly duties" twenty-four hours a day? Or "Christian duties" twenty-four hours a day? No, it's integrated into life. That is the reason I've always loved referring to my career as "a way of life."

When I was first starting my business, a typical day might include taking my kids to school in the mornings, meeting with a customer, having lunch with a friend, making some deliveries, shopping for an hour, picking up my kids, dropping one off at the ball field, dropping another off at piano lessons, making three more deliveries, picking the kids back up, buying them Slurpees, and so on. Now, how much was work and how much was being a mother? Who knows, and who cares? It's all intermingled.

Business owners don't have time clocks to punch, but that doesn't mean you aren't working. It's not as if you'll fire yourself if you don't show up at work! But please don't misunderstand. This is not just about hard work… it's also about *smart* work. The advantage of owning your own business is that you can leverage your time. In the long run, you can make more money with less effort. But you have to put in the hard work to get to that point. It doesn't just happen automatically.

THE #2 KEY:
FIND A FEW GOOD MENTORS

We've been taught all our lives that experience is the best teacher. But that doesn't mean our own experience has to be the best teacher. By the time you gain all the experience you need to live well, you'll be too old, or dead, and you'll never get to use it! We have to learn from the knots on other people's heads, too. We are not going to live long enough to make all the mistakes ourselves. If we're willing to learn from others, we can dramatically decrease the amount of time we spend attending the school of hard knocks.

Another question people frequently ask me is "Who is your mentor?" or "Who was your mentor growing up?" Actually, I didn't have mentors for many, many years because I didn't understand what a mentor was or how valuable one could be. I knew what an idol was. (But even though I grew up in the 1950s, I have to admit I wasn't a big Elvis fan. I thought he was all right, but I wasn't one of those screaming teenage girls who fainted whenever they saw him!) In the early years of my career, we didn't have as many fine examples of successful women as we do today.

When I first heard of the concept of having a mentor, I thought a mentor had to be a person you respected and admired who had it all together. What I have learned, though, is that it's best to have many mentors. I may think of one lady as a mentor because she's gorgeous; it's quite evident by looking at her that she exercises regularly and is disciplined in caring for her appearance. Her self discipline is an example to me. And trust me, physical beauty is the result of regular, disciplined care! If you have gorgeous hair, gorgeous skin, gorgeous nails and a gorgeous body, it is because you worked at it. But this same beautiful lady may have an "attitude" about herself. I may not admire her personality at all.

I may find another lady who is warm and genuine, and I may just love her personality and choose her for a mentor in that respect. But what if she's a slob? Well, I emulate the good and avoid imitating the bad. I may admire another person because she is very strong spiritually, which is very important to me, but if she doesn't have any drive or ambition, I find another mentor for those things.

The point is that I don't need to get everything from one perfect person. I don't believe you're going to find any one person who has it all together. Having many mentors also gives us many different perspectives that broaden our own vision of this world. We get other viewpoints that we didn't already have to discover ourselves.

THE #3 KEY:

THINK BIG AND BE A BIG GOAL-SETTER

Do you know what my favorite definition of goal-setting is? *Setting your sights on getting what you want instead of just wanting what you already have.* Most people go through life trying to convince themselves that they want what they already have because it relieves them of the need to set goals. My friends, you can have anything you want if you learn to set goals and work toward them.

Let me share with you some of the reasons why most people don't set goals. I think one reason is that we've been told the value of goals, but we haven't been *sold* on the value of goals. We don't realize how goals will change and improve our lives. For example, I may be told it's important to drink eight glasses of water a day, but if I haven't been sold on the benefits of drinking water, I won't do it. We can be told we need physical exercise every day, but if we haven't been sold on it, we don't do it. There's a world of difference between "told" and "sold." We won't set goals until we're sold on why we should.

Another reason we don't set goals is simply fear of failure. We fall into the old "what if" game—"What if I do this, and then I fail? What if I reach my goal but can't maintain it? What if I end up with egg on my face? What if I look like a total fool? What if I try and I get rejected? What if, what if, what if...."

Please don't put off living your life because of "what if." None of us has a guarantee for tomorrow, but we do have today. As they say, "It's better to have loved and lost than to never have loved at all."

CHAPTER 8

How Not to Be
Your Own Worst Enemy

I believe the greatest gift you can give yourself and your family is healthy self-esteem. Simply put, self-esteem is how we see ourselves. Without a doubt, how we see ourselves is the most important factor to our success in this life. How other people see us (even though we'd love the whole world to think we're the best thing since sliced bread!) doesn't make a bit of difference in our success or failure. As human beings, we perform according to how we see ourselves. When we change the way we see ourselves, we change our behavior. When we change our behavior, we change our destiny.

People say to me all the time, "Wait a minute, Rena, if I haven't liked myself for fifty years, how come I'm going to start liking myself all of a sudden?" Good question. It's all about how we improve our perception of ourselves.

I'll explain some very specific ways you can improve your

self-esteem.

The first way your self-esteem will improve is by associating with upbeat, excited, and enthusiastic people. Remember, there is a Biblical principle that says, "We become like the people we associate with." If you hang around whiners you'll become a whiner, if you hang around negative folks you'll become negative, and if you hang around people who cuss, cuss words will fall out of your mouth. But here's the good news: If you hang around winners, you'll greatly increase your odds of becoming a *winner!*

Another reason that you'll learn to see yourself more positively is that those same people will constantly be encouraging you. If you are told enough times that you can do something, you actually begin to believe you can! You will become a more outgoing, positive, excited, enthusiastic, goal-setting, positive person this way. A positive self-esteem will dramatically change your life.

We need to learn to look for the good in everybody and in every situation. In other words, "when life gives you a lemon, make lemonade and go on!" Don't worry about what you *don't* have; figure out how to use what you've already got. When you learn to do that, your attitude will change your life, and then you can pass that on to your family. And we all love our families—they are the most important possession that we have in this life.

Now, when it comes to relationships, men are the head of the house, and that is the way the Good Lord intended it.

However, we women are the neck that turns the head. I believe it was Winston Churchill who first said, "The hand that rocks the cradle rules the world." Well, that is also why the saying, "When Mama ain't happy, ain't nobody happy" rings true! Women set the tempo in the home. We have to get our heads on straight so that we, in turn, can pass it on to our families. It's all in our perspective on life.

It's easy to see what a profound impact the ideas we were taught as children have on us as adults. It is our responsibility as parents to train our kids. We need to be their mentors and their heroes. That happens not only by what they have been taught, but also, from another perspective, by what they have *caught,* along the way.

For example, I feel the way I do about Adolph Hitler because of what I learned from my parents and teachers. I obviously didn't know Hitler personally, but I have been told about the horrible atrocities he committed. I believe what I've been taught, and therefore I feel disgust and anger toward him. Because of teachings, I hold beliefs. Beliefs affect my feelings, and my feelings shape my attitude, which in turn determines my actions.

Look at it this way. Let's suppose there are two little children growing up in countries at war with each other—say Iraq and Iran. The children in Iraq are taught that Iran is bad and Iraq is good. At the same time, the children in Iran are taught that Iran is good and Iraq is bad. One day they could shoot at and kill each other, each one believing it is right because he believes what he has been taught.

I'll give you another example. We live in a high-tech computer age, and the computer is a good image of the way our minds work. When you enter information into a computer, it simply accepts whatever is keyed in. It doesn't matter to the computer if it's the truth, fiction, or downright lies—whatever is keyed in, it accepts. And whatever you put in, you get back out. You can't ask a computer to give you something that you haven't given it; it simply can't think for itself.

When we are children, our minds are much like computers. We are vulnerable to all kinds of suggestions, being unable to process critically the things we hear. Fortunately, as we grow older, we become better at thinking for ourselves. And that means re-evaluating some of the things we heard when we were young and impressionable.

We must erase the negative that is in our minds and replace it with something positive. If we only erase and don't replace, we're in trouble. Let me illustrate why.

Let's say I go over to my friend's home (we'll call her Shirley) and see that the place is a disaster. The chairs are falling apart, the couch is moth-eaten, and there isn't a glass in the house that isn't chipped or cracked; in short, it's a mess. So I say, "Shirley, you're my good friend, and I hate to be the one to tell you, but this place is a total fiasco! It breaks my heart to see you living in such a negative environment. Let me help you clean up this mess."

I then take the rest of the day and spend it cleaning with

Shirley. We carry out all the broken junk and stack it in the garage. We spit and polish the house until it sparkles. Finally, I look around and say, "Shirley, your house looks great!" and I pack up and go home.

Shirley looks around the room, and she thinks, "It does look different. This place is really clean." Then she looks around for a place to sit down, but there are no chairs. We took them out of the living room because they were all broken. So she decides she'll go out to the garage and retrieve just one chair. A little while later she's sitting there kind of bored, and she thinks, "You know, that TV wasn't worth much, but it was better than nothing." She gets the old television out of the garage and brings it back in. It won't be long before, little by little, Shirley has dragged everything right back inside there. Why? Because she had nothing with which to replace the old broken stuff that was thrown out.

Think about how different it would have been if, after I helped her throw out all that junk, an eighteen wheeler backed up to her door and delivered gorgeous, new furniture, the prettiest Shirley had ever seen. What if men had brought in chairs, tables, couches for every room, and all the accessories you could ask for, from silk flower arrangements right down to the last decorative candle? Shirley would *never* have gone back to using the junk in her garage.

In the same way, we have to replace our old negative thoughts with positive ones. If we don't, before we can take two breaths the negative starts coming back in. Jesus said that once a demon is cast out of a man, it goes and gets more like itself and brings them back to find the man's soul "swept clean"— but also empty. So the demons set up residence again. Our old ways of thinking do the same, unless we've given our mental space to better residents.

Sometimes we hurt ourselves by relying on someone else to make us happy. How many marriage partners do that? In essence, they say to their spouse, "Your job is to make me happy." But that is just not true. If you're not happy with yourself, your spouse can't make you happy.

Another way to avoid being your own worst enemy is to refuse to make excuses. In business today, there are basically two types of sales people: those who make excuses and those who make money. People who make excuses will never achieve their goals, let alone achieve greatness.

What if Paul Revere had said, "I can't ride and tell all the people the British are coming. Where do you think I'm going to get a horse at this time of night?" Or what if Martin Luther King had said, "You know, I had a dream, but right now I forget what it was." Or what if Jesus had said, "Go and sin no more, unless you have a bad day at work." You see, it's easy to come up with an excuse for why we can't do something. Excuses really do bring out the worst in people. They can lead us to lie, they allow us to avoid taking responsibility for our own lives, and they encourage us to believe we're not in control. *Folks, we have to quit making excuses.*

As much as possible, we should not try to do the impossible, because it is just too frustrating. Now, as you can imagine, I don't place too many things in the category of the impossible. But one impossible, frustrating activity is attempting to make something happen for people who are not willing to make it happen for themselves. Eddie and I have learned a lot through his work as a social worker. We've seen families taken out of pigsties and given nice, clean frame houses. In six months, they're living in a pigsty again.

I've learned the hard way that most people who don't have screens on their windows and doors don't have them because they don't want screens on their windows and doors. They will have a 45" television in their living room, but no screens—and you and I are out raising funds to help them buy screens. Who's the fool?

If someone said to me, "My kids are starving to death, would you give me $50 cash for groceries?" I wouldn't give it to her. I learned the hard way that she'll take that money and buy cigarettes, booze, and nail polish remover, and the kids are lucky if they'll get a Twinkie. Instead I'll load the kids in the car, take them to the grocery store, and buy them what they need. But hand over the cash? No way. It's not good for them, and it's not good for me.

People often ask, "Well, how did you get started in Mary Kay if you were so darned poor?"

The difference is that I was a person who had accepted responsibility for my life. I'm not just talking about not having very much money; I'm talking about being poor because of being irresponsible. I've never had a bill collector at my door. If I owed you $2.50 on the first, you would have your $2.50 on the first. If I couldn't pay you on the first, I never would have borrowed it from you to begin with. I honor my commitments.

When I started with Mary Kay, I was committed to doing the business well. Anyone who was committed to it could have done the same. But so many people stay poor because they are not committed to getting out of poverty. The rich get richer, and the poor get poorer. Is it fair? Yes. Listen carefully to what I'm saying: I'm talking about people who have never accepted responsibility for their own lives. I know I'm on thin ice talking about this—I risk stepping on somebody's toes. But I know you won't be offended if you listen with an open mind.

People get what they are committed to obtaining, whether it is something or nothing. I believe if we took all the money in the world and equally divided it, in two years it would be back in the same hands.

Another way we end up as our own worst enemy is by allowing ourselves to get depressed. Low self-esteem usually leads to depression. One of the best books I've read about depression is called *Happiness Is a Choice*, by Dr. Paul Meier and Dr. Frank Minirth. Depression knows no boundaries—the young, the old, the rich, the poor, the successful, the failures—everyone at some time or another becomes depressed. The sad part is if we ignore the warning signals (the "blues" that we feel at the onset of this malady), then we can't figure out what's wrong and get back in control.

Did you know that today, after car accidents, the number two killer among our young people is suicide? That is heartbreaking. And, of course, the first cause of suicide is depression. It's important to realize that when we have low self-esteem, we are a much more likely candidate for depression than if our self-esteem is high.

And it is not only for our own sakes that we need to have high self-esteem. As we learn in Scripture, we are to love our neighbor as ourselves. Think about that one a minute. It stands to reason that if I don't like *me*, I can't like you. You cannot love your neighbor unless you love yourself. I'm not talking about an egotistical, arrogant, prideful, or selfish love. I'm talking about healthy self-esteem.

Another reason to love yourself is so that you can reach others for the Lord. If you are depressed, poor, stressed out, morbid, and barely existing, who could possibly want what you've got? You're not going to have a chance to affect other people's hearts and souls for Christ unless you are Christ-like yourself. People judge us by what they see first. We've heard all our lives, "Don't judge a book by its cover." But we still do. If the cover doesn't look good, we never flip open the front to see what's inside. Even so, for better or worse, people judge us by appearance.

When I meet someone who is fresh and vibrant, I want to know more about what makes that person tick. I believe with all my heart that those of us who claim to be the children of the Lord ought to be the most successful, the happiest, the most enthusiastic, and the wealthiest people walking the face of this earth!

But is low self-esteem only our problem? Unfortunately, no. One of the disturbing issues of having low self-esteem is its impact on children. Our kids need to see that we believe in ourselves. They learn from us. How can we expect our children to respect us if we don't respect ourselves? It just won't happen. For our children, we are the image of authority and even of God. It stands to reason, then, that if we want them to respect God and authority, we need to present a respectable image.

When we worry about what we'll leave to our children when we die, we often focus on insurance policies, wills, and priceless possessions. These things are all fine and good, but they aren't what's really important. Instead we need to leave to our kids a legacy of respect for God and authority, an enthusiasm for life and healthy self-esteem. When we leave them these things, our children will be just fine no matter what comes along in life. They'll land on their feet and make a positive contribution to this world long after you and I are gone. We need only to give them the right tools.

Apologizing all the time is one sure way to reinforce a negative self-image. Many of the phrases that we use regularly, we probably haven't even thought of as being negative; in fact, we might even be convinced they are hallmarks of humility. Many times we start out negatively by apologizing, "I know I could have done this project better." "I'm sorry. I apologize for not being prepared tonight." When we start out our conversation with an apology we're essentially saying, "I'm not good at what I'm doing." When someone asks you to do something, and you respond by saying, "Well, I'm not sure I can do it, but I guess I'll give it a try," what do you think happens to her confidence in you? It all but disappears.

Often I hear women convey self-doubt with a voice inflection, turning a statement into a question. It's almost as though they're back to asking daddy permission to do something. They say things like, "Can I get back with you?" instead of saying, "I'll get back with you." Do you hear the difference? These little killer phrases help destroy self-esteem.

We have to learn to ask for what we want. Until you develop a healthy self-esteem, you can't ask for the raise you deserve or whatever else it is you need.

I was speaking in Des Moines, Iowa, one night. After the meeting ended, I was at the back of the room greeting everybody and a lovely, older gentleman came up to one of the ladies there and said, "You look like my third wife." She was caught rather off guard and said, "How many times have you been married?" He looked at her with a mischievous sparkle in his eyes and said, "Twice!"

That is asking for what you want, isn't it? Many people need to learn to be more assertive. One of the reasons I believe women in particular don't want to be assertive is that they associate it with being pushy, impolite, and just plain obnoxious. But there is a difference between being assertive and being aggressive. The first definition listed in the dictionary for aggressive is, "Inclined to behave in a hostile fashion." The definition for assertive, on the other hand, is, "Inclined to bold or confident assertion." The key is being self-assured. Developing healthy self-esteem helps us to become more self-assured and take more control of our lives.

We all talk to ourselves even though we may not think we do. When you think to yourself "I'm tired" or "I have a headache," you are talking to yourself. We all know words can be devastating, especially when spoken to ourselves. That is why it's so important to be careful about what you say to yourself. Words such as, "I'm fat," "I'm clumsy," "I'm no good at math," "I never do anything right," or "There's no way I'm ever going to fit back in those clothes," become self-fulfilling prophecies. Make a conscious effort to listen to yourself either in your head or when you're talking to friends or clients. You may be surprised to hear what is coming out of your mouth!

Talking to ourselves can be good. Many of our beautiful hymns are examples of someone talking to himself. The 23rd Psalm is written that way. "The Lord is my shepherd. I shall not want..."

One of the best ways we can replace negative thoughts is by reading good books.

Now I can almost hear you saying, "You're crazy, Rena. I don't have time to think, much less read a book!" Well, like most things in life that are worth doing, it takes discipline to read. Even if it's just ten minutes in the morning or before you go to sleep at night, get out at least one book and start reading (and I'm not talking about Danielle Steele's latest romance novel, ladies!). I'm talking about books that will help you open up your mind and tap your potential. Reading needs to be a daily part of your life!

I want to recommend a few more books that I think you will really enjoy. One is *What to Say When You Talk to Yourself,* by Shad Helmstetter. *How to Be Your Own Best Friend,* by Mildred Newman is a great book, as is *Living Above the Level of Mediocrity,* by Chuck Swindoll, one of my very favorite authors.

Remember, never put yourself down, even jokingly. When you put yourself down, it leaves a lasting impression—not just on other people but on *you!* Your subconscious mind (remember the computer up in our head) accepts most of what it hears, whether it's truth or fiction.

One tool you can use to build your self-esteem is positive affirmation. You can rewrite your familiar scripts instead of expressing yourself in the negative: turn the "I can't possibly do that" into "I can." In doing so, you fool the subconscious. It's exactly what the advertising media does; they fool our subconscious through repetition. Our mind has two dimensions that are neither mystical nor hokey: the conscious and the subconscious. Whatever we feed into that subconscious, it will accept and believe. And don't forget, we get out what we put in.

That is why it is essential to make a concerted effort to say things to yourself that are positive. "I look at life optimistically, and I am eager to accept new challenges" or, "I enjoy receiving compliments."

It amazes me that many women don't know how to take a compliment. Not being able to accept a compliment stems from low self-esteem. It truly saddens me to hear so many women start tearing themselves down automatically if someone says, "I love your hair." Instead of a gracious "Thank you," they reply "Oh my gosh, if I don't get these roots fixed..." Or if someone says, "I love your dress," they'll retort, "This old thing? I've had this for years." If you've been talking to yourself negatively, it may take a while to break the habit, but give it a shot. I've heard so many men say they wish women would learn to say thank you and keep their mouths shut instead of trying to explain it!

A simple way to begin to turn a degrading thought around is to affirm its opposite. Let's say, for example, that one of your weak points is not taking time on a daily basis to be grateful. Instead of affirming the negative statement, "You know, I don't take time to count my blessings or even pray as I should," turn it around and state it in the positive: "I take time every day to count my blessings." Remember, when we say something positive, we're actually informing the subconscious. That is one of the best ways to build self-esteem. If you keep telling yourself you're valuable, pretty soon you're going to believe it. *You are valuable!* Once you begin to believe it, you're going to perform accordingly.

Take time to write some affirmations for yourself. When I first began doing this, the way I remembered to read them on a regular basis was to write them down on a piece of paper and put it in my pillowcase. When I would lay down at night to go to sleep, the paper would crinkle, and I would say, "Ah, my affirmations." I would whip them out and read them, and then I would lay them right on the floor. When I got up in the morning, the first thing my feet would hit were my affirmations. I would pick them up, read them again and put them back in the pillowcase. That way, even if I didn't think about them again, at least I was reading them out loud twice a day.

Now, your husband may think you're nuts, unless you get him into reading his own affirmations! Remember, it's okay to be a little nuts; besides, it definitely won't matter when you're laughing all the way to the bank!

Another thing that we have to remember as we build our self-esteem is that you're not going to please *everybody*. I guess that has been one of the hardest lessons for me. It's probably been hard because I want others' love and approval. The bottom line is, I want to be seen as perfect in their eyes even though I know I'm not perfect, and I know I can't please everybody. Yet the human side of me still wants approval and love. We all have to realize that we can't please everybody. The higher up the ladder you go in this life, the more criticism you're going to receive. When everyone can see you, you're a much more obvious target.

Bill Cosby once said, "I may not know the key to success, but I do know the sure way to failure is to try to please everybody!"

Just remember, we *can't* please everybody. We cannot be all things to all people, and we have to accept that. If you change completely, those who liked you before won't like you now! But if you believe in yourself, you won't be devastated when you haven't pleased somebody. Trying to please everyone is impossible.

Unfortunately, people *are* going to talk about you. It's sad but true. *If people think it, they're going to say it.* You're not going to stop them. Somewhere right now, there are some people sitting around talking about you! Keep in mind, how we see ourselves is so much more important than how others see us.

Sometimes it can be hard to keep a good attitude when the pressures of everyday life are all around you. One of my very favorite ways to encourage and teach myself is through audiotapes. Audiotapes are a powerful, convenient way to get invaluable information. I cherish my tape library even more than my book library because, bottom line, I use it more. You can listen to a tape while you are driving down the road, cooking dinner, taking your bath, or putting on your make-up. There's no reason we can't listen to a tape while we are doing something else. All you have to do is to push a button. I don't care if it takes you five minutes, twenty minutes, or an hour to get ready in the morning, use that time to move yourself forward in life. Listening to a tape will rev you up for the day. Then, when the disappointments come (and they will!), you can deal with them and handle them because you're prepared. But if you're not feeling "up" already, you begin to sink lower and lower until, before you know it, you're way down in the pits.

That is why it's imperative for you to listen to tapes every day! If I were to ask a typical group of people if they listen to tapes every single day, only a small percentage would respond positively.

Yet, I have never known anyone who listened to tapes every day of their life who wasn't successful. The flip side of the coin is that I've never known anyone who was successful for very long (there is a difference between long-term success versus short-term success) who didn't listen to tapes on a regular basis. It's crucial, but it's such a simple little thing.

The good news is that as our self-esteem improves, we can sit back and see the lighter side of life. We become far less self-conscious and can laugh at ourselves more easily. I do a great deal of public speaking all over the country, and sometimes the introductions I get are really funny. One time I was in Buffalo, New York, sitting on stage all ready to share some of my pearls of wisdom when the host got up to introduce me. I stood up and walked over to the podium with him. The PA system in the auditorium was having some trouble but had been sufficiently repaired for us to begin. So when the host got up to the microphone, he said, "I want to apologize for our speaker tonight—it has a loose screw." The crowd looked at me standing there and cracked up laughing!

On another occasion someone got up and said, "I want to introduce our speaker tonight, Rena Tarbet. By the way, that reminds me of a joke."

It *never* hurts to be able to laugh at yourself!

CHAPTER 9

Making Money Is
Not Only Okay—It's Great!

One of my favorite sayings is: Money doesn't buy happiness, but it does buy *choices.*

Do you want to feed the Third World? It takes money. Do you want to sponsor a missionary full-time on foreign soil? It takes money. Do you want to send your kids and your grandkids to the colleges of their choice? It takes money. Do you want to be able to take care of your aging parents? It takes money. Do you want to be able to lie in the sun in Hawaii (with your sunscreen on, of course!)? It takes money.

When you make enough money, you can live where you want and do what you want when you want. If you don't make enough money, you don't have a choice. You have to get up and go to work tomorrow, like it or not. Money is one means of getting what you want out of life.

I love to talk about money for two major reasons. First, I

am highly motivated by money. I don't mind saying that—it's true! I figure that people who say that money doesn't motivate them lie about other things, too!

The second reason I like to talk about money is that it's probably one of the most misunderstood subjects in the world today. You know, people amaze me. They'll loan you their car, they'll loan you their Mont Blanc pen, they'll even loan you their wife before they'll loan you money! You start talking money, and they start backing up, afraid you're going to ask for some of theirs.

You see, more of us grew up poor than grew up wealthy. If our parents couldn't give us a whole lot materially speaking, they just taught us it wasn't important. That was the end of our training about money. (It wasn't exactly a well-rounded financial education!) They said, "It's what's on the inside that counts, not the outside." I know that is true, but I'm going to tell you something—the outside is pretty darn important, too! Ninety percent of what I see on your outside, *you bought*—the clothes you have on and the makeup you're wearing. Some of you even bought the color of your hair (and there are those of us who bought the hair itself!).

Money is important, but our parents didn't teach us that. To add insult to injury, if you grew up poor materially and strong spiritually (I did and will be eternally grateful that I grew up strong spiritually!), then you got a double whammy.

Remember all those sayings we grew up with? "Money is the root of all evil," "Money is filthy lucre," "Money is cold, hard cash," "It's easier for a camel to go through the eye of a needle than it is for a rich man to go to heaven." As children, we tried to visualize all this and decided we sure didn't want to be rich.

Like I said, I grew up very, very poor. My parents went through the Depression, we kids were born during the war, and we didn't have many material possessions. I grew up in a Christian family in a home that was very rich in love and very poor in material things. But somewhere along the line we were taught a lot of principles that weren't true, including that there is righteousness in poverty. That is not a Biblical principle, and yet a lot of us were brought up believing that. Maybe it wasn't taught in so many words, but it was implied.

When someone drove by in a Cadillac my parents would say, "Wonder what kind of trouble they've been up to?" That was the underlying thought about people who were successful or wealthy, and this is simply a wrong attitude.

However, if you loved the Lord and were broke, it was okay because you had God on your side. Listen: Money isn't filthy, and it's not cold and hard. It's warm, it's soft, and it's good. Money isn't the root of all evil. If you're going to quote the Good Book, then by all means, quote it right. It says in 1 Timothy 6:10, "For the *love of money* is a root of all kinds of evil, for which some have strayed from the faith in their greediness, and pierced themselves through with many sorrows."

It's when money becomes our idol or our god that it's wrong. Money is good. It pays hospital bills, it educates your kids and mine, it sends missionaries to foreign soil, and it takes care of homeless kids, battered wives and aged parents. Money is good! The bottom line is this: first, make a lot of money. Second, give God the credit, the honor, and the glory (in and of ourselves we are nothing). And finally, use it wisely.

When we do that, God will richly bless us. I learned a long time ago that we can't out-give God. We have a little bitty shovel—He has a great big one. The more we shovel out for others, the more He shovels back.

ATTITUDES ABOUT MONEY AND MAKING SALES IN YOUR BUSINESS

Just like everybody else I had some hang-ups. In the middle of my career, I was busy working to build a top unit in the company. I had three teenagers in junior and senior high school. Every day of the week I was working diligently at keeping a balance in my life. I was taking chemotherapy fourteen days a month, and I simply didn't have enough hours in the day to do all I had to do.

In the middle of all this, it became apparent that I had a hang-up about married women making career decisions without asking their husbands. I just believed women wouldn't sign an agreement without asking permission. So I was doing all of my recruiting interviews at night or on the weekends, when I could see couples instead of just wives. I was out of time and frustrated.

In an attempt to relieve this frustration, I took a poster board, and I kept records for one year. I wrote down the names of all the women I interviewed that year, including whether they were married or not. If they were married, were their husbands present at the time of the interview? I wrote down whether I got the money at the time of the interview. I also wrote down how much initial inventory they started with and where they were one year later.

What a valuable learning experience that was. I learned that, no, a woman does not have to ask her husband to make a decision worth $100 or less—which is how much it costs to join Mary Kay. I can go to the grocery store for a gallon of milk and a loaf of bread and end up spending that much money! Women all over the country do that without ever asking permission. And we do it week after week.

I've come to the conclusion that if a woman can't make a $100 decision without asking her husband, I'm not sure I *want* her involved in my business. It's doubtful she'll ever be independent enough to make it.

Please don't be offended by what I'm saying. Can you see me going shopping and finding a dress I want and having to call Eddie to see if it's okay for me to get it? I can almost hear you laughing! It's funny, isn't it? But what's the difference? If we can't make $100 decisions without consulting our husbands, our marriage already has problems that go beyond mere finances.

The second thing I learned from that chart was that if I

didn't close a sale at the time of the interview, I rarely ever got another chance. So I said to myself, "Tarbet, you'd better learn how to close." So I went to work. I learned when to lean in and when to lean back, when to touch and when not to touch, when to raise my voice and when to lower it, when to put an agreement in their hands and when to hand them a pen. I really worked at it.

For some reason, it seems as if people today don't want to work at getting good. They want to buy into the company, flip through a guide, hit the streets, and be a pro. Then when it doesn't happen, they get frustrated and say, "Well, God's trying to tell me something. I should have stayed where I was."

Many of us have spent years becoming teachers, nurses, CPAs, attorneys, executive secretaries, or whatever. We've spent many years in school, and many thousands of dollars, working at becoming good. The same applies when we start something new. You have to work at being good. If you don't like what you are doing, get out! But if you're going to do it, then hey, you're here by choice, so why not be a pro? It pays much better. You'll have a lot more fun and much less stress.

I'll never forget one lesson I learned early in my career. I recruited a lady, and I assumed that she could not afford to start with more than the minimum amount of wholesale product, so that is all I told her about. When she found out a few weeks later that she could have started with much more inventory, she was not only disappointed, she was angry with me. She shook her finger in my face—I'll never forget it—and said, "You have no right to make my decisions for me." And I said, "Yes ma'am. You're right, and I was wrong. I apologize, and I will never make that mistake again." My friends, I never have!

Anytime I share a business opportunity with anybody, anywhere, I'm going to explain all the options just as honestly and up-front as I know how to be. I'm going to tell you every choice you have from A to Z, and then I'm going to put the ball back in your court and say, "Now, the decision is yours. I will help you whatever you choose, but I'm not going to vote for you. That part is up to you."

The point I want to make is this: don't be afraid to treat your business like a business. I work with career-minded women for the most part. They want and need to know how to make money. When I give a sales presentation, the first thing I talk about is how we sell an incredible product. I use that four-letter word: *S-E-L-L.*

I believe with all my heart that selling is the greatest profession in the world! Unfortunately, we've had too much negative conditioning about selling. Your high school teachers and your college professors didn't encourage you to go into sales, did they? "Selling" wasn't even considered a profession. It was like a last resort: those who can, do; those who can't, sell something. Selling was for the untalented or the uneducated. Sales people were always pictured as a nuisance. "There's another pesky salesman on the phone." "That silver-tongued devil of a salesman talked me into such-and-such."

We grew up believing that to be good in sales we had to be outgoing, loud-mouthed, aggressive, and dominant. If that was not the kind of person we wanted to be, then a career in sales was out of the question.

Fortunately, the approach to selling and the concept of the salesperson are changing for the better. As a practical matter, the *only* way to build a permanent career in selling is to have solid character and integrity.

What, then, is selling? Selling is a transferring of your beliefs. If you believe in what you are promoting—whether it's an idea or a product—and you have the ability to get along with people, and behave in a warm, friendly manner, you can be at the top in sales! It doesn't matter whether you're an introvert or an extrovert. It's okay to be whoever you are.

You may not initially think your particular "style" will be successful in sales. There are many different types of people in the world, however. There are many people who are turned off by an aggressive sales person. An introverted person may come in with a sweet, calm, low-key manner and close them easily—precisely because of their style of selling. We can all be good in sales if we believe in what we are promoting and if we enjoy being around people.

I can show you all types of sales people at the top of the ladder, whether in the automobile industry, insurance, real estate, cosmetics, or whatever. You are who you're supposed to be. Don't use "I'm not the sales type" as an excuse because "it takes all types to sell to all types!"

One of the greatest fears people have is a fear of rejection. This is especially true of people in sales. Yet, the worst thing a prospect can do is say they don't want what you're selling. You have a choice when they say "no"—you can either call them again, or never see them again.

Another common reason people think they can't be successful in sales is that they just don't have time. I love hearing that one, and I'll tell you why.

First off, I *choose* to be a very busy person. To be honest with you, I don't know anybody walking the earth who is busier than I am. That is not complaining or boasting—it's just a fact. I learned a long time ago that busy people are the happiest people and the most successful. They are the movers and the shakers. They have places to go, things to do, and people to see.

They're not moaning, groaning, whining, and complaining. They don't have headaches and backaches—they don't have time for that.

So how do they do it all? There are two things you need to understand.

First, time doesn't move at different rates for different people. We all have the same amount of time. God gives all of us 168 hours a week. He is no respecter of persons. Isn't it amazing how some people get so much done and others are still "fixin' to get started"? To get things done, it takes not only drive and ambition; it also takes time management and organization. We all get the same amount of time per day, but it's how we choose to use it that makes *all the difference!*

Second, we have to understand that when we really believe something is important, we will take the time to do it, whether it's going to church, exercising daily or whatever. If you are really sold on the value of a particular thing, you will invest time in it. It's as simple as that.

CHAPTER 10

Choose a Destination
and Get Moving

I have a question I would like to ask you. The question is: What do you want from life?

No one can tell us what we want. No one can set our goals for us. Sure, people can give us guidance, and they can tell us how to set goals, but we have to decide for ourselves what we want. And we have to keep in mind that what we want to *do* and what we want to *be* are two distinct goals. No matter what you do in life, it is not an end in itself. It is a means to an end. It can be a vehicle to help you become what you want to be, which in turn can be an end in itself, provided you are wise in choosing that goal.

Your goals may not be specifically about money. My husband, Eddie, is a very happy individual. He has four years of college, seminary training, and a master's degree in social work, and his career has always been oriented toward serving others. His goal is not about making a lot of money. We have a beautiful, million-dollar home, and when we bought it fifteen years ago I was taking chemo and not expected to live. People thought I was crazy! They were saying, "Rena, what if you don't make it? What if you die, and he's left with this house? What if...?"

Frankly, we don't think like that in our home, thank you very much! I'll probably be the ninety-year-old lady who takes out a thirty-year loan! I don't worry about "what if." A "what if" mentality limits the way you live your life. You're missing out on so many of the rewards and riches of life that way!

Believe it or not, one of the seemingly strange reasons many people don't set goals is fear of *success*. Did you know that fear of success is a greater fear than fear of failure? I didn't believe that when I was first taught it, but I've studied it, I've researched it and it's a fact.

For many people, the number one fear of success is that there are going to be a lot of folks that just plain don't like them *because* they're successful. And they're right. There will be! The more successful we become, the more average folks think we are "showing them up."

People will often let their circumstances define them as a "victim." It seems that almost everybody today loves a victim story. When people tell their victim stories, we just huddle around them; we can't wait for them to finish so we can tell ours! But when your victim stories start to be replaced with success stories, people are not sure they like you so much anymore. Your "aliveness" makes their "deadness" more apparent. There are a lot of dead folks in this world! Oh, they're still moving around, but they're dead. Have you ever looked into somebody's eyes and seen that there was nobody home? Those are the people I'm talking about!

You may have family and friends right now who are uncomfortable with your excitement and enthusiasm and how you're changing. They (usually unintentionally) say things that can make you feel guilty: "You used to have time to have coffee with me or go shopping, but now all you do is work, work, work." They'll try to put you on a guilt trip *big time* because you're doing well. You have chosen to grow, and they haven't. The more successful you become, the more you are going to outgrow things and people.

When we are growing and becoming successful, our priorities change. In my earlier days, I was a "Jill of all trades," so to speak. I could out-decoupage just about anybody, I did crewel embroidery, stripped down ugly old pieces of furniture and made beautiful antiques out of them, made jelly, froze corn, and made pickles. I'm even a seamstress—I used to make all of Eddie's suits.

My goals are different now. I don't do any of those things anymore, and I never will again. Does that make me a bad person? Of course not. They served a time, a place, and a purpose in my life. I have outgrown them, and it's okay.

It helps to be prepared for things to change. When you're successful, you're going to have people that criticize you for some of your changes. It just comes with the territory. As much as we may want to be "Superwoman," we simply can't do it all. When we have limited time and energy, something has to give!

I can't work with customers, go to sales meetings every week, go to church three times a week, make homemade jelly, attend nine ball games a week, collect for the neighborhood cancer drive, organize the neighborhood garage sale, play bridge twice a week, sing in the choir, teach Sunday School, go to Ladies Bible Class, and be campaign chairman for the city councilman.

Since I can't do it all, I have to decide what's important and what's not. What are my priorities? I have to please the Good Lord and my family. It's important to remember that. If PTA is important to your kids, go—and if it is not, don't you dare go just because somebody else thinks you "ought" to!

Another reason we don't set goals is that we don't know how. So let me give you several suggestions that have been helpful to me on how to set goals.

First, you must be very, very specific about what you want. You can't be generic when you set goals. It doesn't help to want a big house, want to be very successful, or want to make lots of money. Those goals are too generic. What exactly is a big house? To some people 2,500 square feet is a big house, and to someone else, nothing less than ten thousand square feet will do. You say you want lots of money? Some people would think $20,000 a year is a lot of money, but for other people it would take $50,000. There are some people who need to have a six-figure income to feel that they are making a good salary. That is why you have to be very specific.

Second, your goals absolutely must be written down. I get so tickled when people say, "Oh, I know what I want; it's right here in my head." No! It has to be written down in black and white. Place your written goals in strategic places where you'll see them all the time. Write them on a big poster that you hang up in your office or in your home. Make a smaller duplicate that you carry with you, maybe in your date book or in a spiral notebook. Write it on three-by-five cards and hang them where you spend the most time—the refrigerator, the telephone, the dashboard, and the bathroom mirror.

Put pictures of the things that are important to you on the poster and in your day planner. I live out of my day planner/date book. The first three pages are pictures of my husband and children, my mom and dad—even my dog is in there. My family is such a vital part of my life; they motivate me daily. I want to have the time and the money to do anything I want with and for them. I work hard on a daily basis because I know what I want, and I want it badly enough to pay the price.

I'll share three of my fun goals with you. I carry them around with me all the time. I'm going to:

- Take my grandkids to the Olympics.
- Take my granddaughters shopping in Paris.
- Take my grandsons to the Super Bowl.

Remember: money buys choices, not happiness. Don't

ever forget that principle. We all know rich people who aren't happy. The reason money can't make you happy is that true happiness is from within. But even so, I'd rather be happy and rich than happy and poor!

I refuse to let anything keep me from achieving my goals. It's important that we all learn to achieve our goals regardless of what's going on in our lives. I think of myself as a mouse in a little maze who, instead of going through all the twists and turns, simply blows right through the walls, arriving at the goal. You see, I know my purpose in life, I know God's purpose for me, and I believe I'm living according to it. I'm not going to let anybody or anything stop me when I know I'm right. That is determination.

Another one of my favorite sayings has always been, "When your determination to succeed is strong enough, failure will never overtake you." Isn't that comforting? I cling to that when things aren't going right. You know, there are times when it just seems like no matter what I do, nothing's going right. When you're determined, however, you'll find a way over, under, around, or through.

Next, your goals have to have a deadline. When you say, "I'm going to be a millionaire someday," my response is "Whoop-de-do." I mean, "someday" is not a day of the week! You have to be specific about time.

When setting deadlines, it's important not to set them too far away. If it's January and I say I'm going to lose ten pounds by July, I'll probably think, "Why start now?" It's likely I won't *start* until June! Six months is too far off. We don't stay motivated for long periods at a time (I think we women are worse than men on that one!). It would be better for me to decide to lose two pounds by February; then, in February, I can set a goal for March, and so forth. When you set your long-term goals, it is helpful to break them up into short-term goals. It takes little successes to get to the big successes. And the more little successes we get under our belt, the better the odds that we will reach the big ones. Accomplishments increase confidence. If you're not confident enough, one of the ways to build your confidence is through accomplishments.

Knowledge also builds our confidence. The more knowledge we have on a given subject, the more confident we will be in that area. So it is a good idea to learn all we can about the things we want to do.

All right, let's say we've done all that. Let's say we've written our goals out in detail, we've set deadlines, we've learned all we can about them—now why wouldn't we reach our goals once we've set them? Let me give you a few of the reasons why we stop short of success.

WE JUST FLAT
HAVE A ROTTEN ATTITUDE

Although I believe faith is the beginning point of everything, attitude comes in a close second! Here's a story I heard from a friend that I think illustrates the kind of attitude we should have.

"Jerry" was in the food service business. He was the kind of guy you love to hate. He was always in a good mood and always had something positive to say. When someone would ask him how he was doing, he would reply, "If I were any better, I would be twins!"

He was a unique manager because he had several waiters who had followed him around from restaurant to restaurant. The reason the waiters followed Jerry was his attitude. He was a natural motivator. If an employee was having a bad day, Jerry would tell the employee how to look on the positive side of the situation.

Seeing this style really made me curious, so one day I went up to Jerry and said, "I don't get it. You can't be a positive person all of the time. How do you do it?" Jerry replied, "Each morning I wake up and say to myself, 'Jerry, you have two choices today. You can choose to be in a good mood, or you can choose to be in a bad mood.' I choose to be in a good mood. Each time something bad happens, I can choose to be a victim or I can choose to learn from it. I choose to learn from it. Every time someone comes to me complaining, I can choose to accept their complaining or I can point out the positive side of life. I choose the positive side of life."

"Yeah, right, it's not that easy," I protested. "Yes, it is," Jerry said. "Life is all about choices. When you cut away all the junk, every situation is a choice. You choose how you react to situations. You choose how people will affect your mood. You choose to be in a good mood or a bad mood. The bottom line is: It's your choice how you live life."

I reflected on what Jerry said. Soon thereafter, I left the restaurant industry to start my own business. We lost touch, but I often thought about him when I made a choice about life instead of reacting to it.

Several years later, I heard that Jerry did something you are never supposed to do in a restaurant business: he left the back door open one morning and was held up at gunpoint by three armed robbers. While trying to open the safe, his hand, shaking from nervousness, slipped off the combination. The robbers panicked and shot him. Providentially, Jerry was found relatively quickly and rushed to the local trauma center. After eighteen hours of surgery and weeks of intensive care, Jerry was released from the hospital with fragments of the bullets still in his body.

I saw Jerry about six months after the accident. When I asked him how he was, he replied, "If I were any better, I would be twins. Wanna see my scars?"

I declined to see his wounds, but I did ask him what had gone through his mind as the robbery took place. "The first thing that went through my mind was that I should have locked the back door," Jerry replied. "Then, as I lay on the floor, I remembered that I had two choices: I could choose to live or I could choose to die. I chose to live."

"Weren't you scared? Did you lose consciousness?" I asked.

Jerry continued, "The paramedics were great. They kept telling me I was going to be fine. But when they wheeled me into the ER, and I saw the expressions on the faces of the doctors and nurses, I got really scared. In their eyes I read, 'He's a dead man.' I knew I needed to take action."

"What did you do?" I asked.

"Well, there was a big, burly nurse shouting questions at me," said Jerry. "She asked if I was allergic to anything. 'Yes,' I replied. The doctors and nurses stopped working as they waited for my reply. I took a deep breath and yelled, 'Bullets!' Over their laughter, I told them, 'I am choosing to live. Operate on me as if I am alive, not dead.'"

Jerry lived not only because of the skill of his doctors but also because of his amazing attitude. I learned from him that every day we have to choose to live life fully.

WE DON'T WANT
IT BADLY ENOUGH

As you know, I took chemotherapy for six consecutive years. I reached the point where I would rather be tied to a stake and beaten to a pulp than take chemo any longer. I hated it. In some ways I think chemotherapy is tougher on adults than kids because kids don't have to make the choice to take the chemotherapy, they don't get to vote, even though our hearts break for them because they don't understand why they have to go through it. Yet, it was very tough for me because I *did* have to vote. Every three weeks I had to ask myself, "Tarbet, are you going back for the next round?" Nobody could make me. I had to make that decision myself.

The reason I did it is that I desperately wanted to live. When you want something badly enough, you will do whatever it takes to get it. How badly do you want to achieve your goal? You have to want something pretty seriously to make a definite decision about it.

I love the Nike commercial that says, "Just do it." Don't spend a lot of time analyzing. Too much analysis causes paralysis! Don't wait until you are inspired. Go to work, and you'll *be* inspired.

A professional artist doesn't wait until he's "inspired" to sit down and paint. No, he throws away lots of canvases before the masterpiece emerges. An author throws away many pages of a manuscript before she has her novel. Remember: *perspiration creates inspiration.*

If you only work in your business when you feel like it, the likelihood of your making it is slim to none. You can't run it on emotions. Remember: emotions lie.

WE DON'T REACH OUR GOALS
BECAUSE WE DON'T CHART OUR PROGRESS

Every Friday I get on an airplane and travel around the country speaking to women. Without exception, after I get on the plane the pilot routinely comes on the air and says, "Ladies and gentlemen, this is your captain speaking. Today we are going to Boston, and our flying time is three hours and thirteen minutes. We're looking at smooth skies, so sit back and enjoy your trip."

So I do. I don't give it another thought. I know that in three hours and thirteen minutes I'm going to be where I'm suppose to be.

Now I would be one upset lady if three hours and thirteen minutes later the captain came on the air and said, "Ladies and gentlemen, this is your captain speaking. We are now in San Diego. Sorry, I missed Boston." Ahhh! I would be upset even if he said, "Ladies and gentlemen, we are now in Newark. I came pretty close!"

Do you know why that doesn't happen? The pilot has an instrument panel that tells him of his progress. It doesn't matter whether it's raining, sleeting or pitch black outside. If he can't see out the windshield, he flies by his instruments. If he gets a tad off target, he immediately—that is the operative word here—makes the adjustments necessary to get right back on target. Three hours and thirteen minutes later he is exactly where he said he would be.

Now, why don't you and I do that? We get all fired up, and off we go. Then the day-to-day living sets in: Johnny failed his algebra test, your mother-in-law is terminally ill and moved in, Susie didn't make cheerleader and is crying hysterically, your husband got laid off, the dog threw up. Day-to-day living causes us to totally lose sight of our goals if we neglect to check our progress regularly. Any time you check your progress and find that you're not on target, ask yourself why. I said this is what I wanted—did I mean it? When I lay my head on the pillow tonight, have I reached my daily goal?

To stay on target for your goal, you have to figure out what is getting you off target. I'm a firm believer that we must identify the problem before we can fix it. I need to identify it today so that tomorrow night when I go to bed, I'm not saying the same thing: "Missed again."

WE DON'T WORK WITH SINGLENESS OF PURPOSE

Distractions can be very costly. Sometimes the only way to move forward is to put blinders on. The reason horses wear blinders in races is so they are not distracted by what's going on around them. That's the whole purpose of blinders.

A woman I was working with was trying to make the "Half Million Dollar Club" in sales. Halfway toward this goal, she purchased a new home—not brand new, but new to her. After moving in she came to me and said, "That wallpaper in the dining room is driving me *crazy.*" It was really outdated, yucky wallpaper. I said, "Well, just don't look at it. We don't have time to go look in wallpaper books, select wallpaper samples or find somebody to do it." She wasn't even thinking of doing it herself, but just finding somebody to do it would have taken a lot of time—time away from her goal of making half a million dollars in the next quarter. So I asked her: "What do you really want? Do you want wallpaper or the Half Million Dollar Club?"

She chose the Half Million Club! You have to put the blinders on to reach your goal. That doesn't mean you can't go back to those things later. She got her wallpaper right after she reached her goal.

You can light a fire with a magnifying glass, but only if you keep it focused on one spot. Keeping your focus may mean you have to give up going to the lake every weekend or baking your own bread or playing tennis. It doesn't mean those things are wrong. It's just that there's a price to be paid. There is no such thing as a free lunch. You give up something to gain something. It's like giving up chocolate cake to lose weight. If you don't give it up, you'll never get thinner. It doesn't take a rocket scientist to figure that out.

The rewards and the benefits are in direct proportion to the effort you exert. There's a truism in life and in work—that when you put in the effort, you get results; if you don't put in any effort, you don't get any results. It's a simple axiom: You are the one who has to decide. And the soul-searching question you have to ask yourself is, "Do I want it badly enough to give something up for the time being?"

My heart goes out to single parents today. They have distractions enough to keep five people off track. It has to be very difficult. I don't know that from experience since I've never been a single mom, but I know it's got to be a tough, tough role. You work a forty-hour week. Every day you have to pick up your kids from the day care center, bring them home and feed them a bologna sandwich. Then you either drop them off with another sitter or have somebody come to the house and keep them while you go out to a sales meeting or sell product to your customers. But just hang in there. It is worth it!

When I was taking chemo, there were days when I felt like throwing in the towel. Oftentimes, the only reason I could continue was that I believed there was an end in sight. I would be finished with the treatment and I would get well. I could keep taking chemotherapy because I never lost sight of the fact that this, too, would pass. I never lost hope. You see, if we get on a downward spiral of thinking there is no hope, we get depressed. Depression is a real thing. However, we can prevent ourselves from getting in that state if we can realize that there is light at the end of the tunnel, and we're taking positive action to correct the situation, whatever it might be.

Now, I hope I'm never tested, but I'm the kind of person who I think could survive being in prison for twenty years. The reason I think I could survive is that I've learned to focus on my goal. If I were locked in prison, I would say, "I've only got nineteen years, 364 days to go." The next day I would say, "I've only got nineteen years, 363 days to go." The next day I would say, "I've only got nineteen years, 362 days." And so on. I would focus on the end of the situation. That's working with singleness of purpose.

The shorter the time frame in which you are trying to reach your goal, the greater the sense of urgency and singleness of purpose must be. For example, if I have a month to lose weight before I can fit into a dress for a wedding, I have to work more diligently than if I've got a year. That's why it's easier to get the weight off in a month than it is in a year. Why? As I said, a year is too far off for me to stay motivated. When I lose sight of my goal, I start rationalizing. We can rationalize ourselves into or out of anything we want. I could start saying, "Actually, I don't look that bad." My friends may even say, "You don't really need to lose weight. You look fine just the way you are." As long as I avoid looking in mirrors when I'm naked, and wear long-tailed jackets, I can probably convince myself that I don't have to worry about fitting into that dress—especially since I've got a whole year to do it. We constantly play little games in our minds. And that's exactly why we lose the big battles.

Of course, it depends on the amount of weight one has to lose. A month may not be a realistic goal. I've heard Zig Ziglar say that despite the fact that he had lost over two thousand pounds in the past, he was still overweight because he took it off on crash diets. Then in 1973, he lost thirty-seven pounds on a gradual basis by sensible eating and exercise, taking off 1.9 ounces per day on the average. In ten months, the 37 pounds were lost—permanently!

WE DON'T WORK WITH CONSISTENCY

Another reason we don't meet our goals is we don't work consistently. We're hot, we're cold. We're on, we're off. We're full speed ahead, and we're dead stop. That is how most people work. Zoom. Eeeeck. Zoom. Eeeeck. Zoom. Eeeeck. I call them *Zoomeeeckers*. They give it everything they've got for a week, and then they take off three weeks because they are so tired. What have they proven except that they can last a week?

Consistency makes an extraordinary impact on reaching our goals. I would rather have a lady who will consistently work three nights a week—week in, week out—than a lady who will work a killer week, take off three weeks, hold a semi-killer week, then skip two, etc. Even if at the end of the year they were even in their overall statistics and performance, I guarantee you the consistent one will be higher up the ladder of success than the other for one reason: momentum.

Momentum is a difficult word to define. It's a fact that if a locomotive is just sitting on a train track and you put a block of wood under its wheels, it can't go anywhere. When that same locomotive is going down the track at ninety miles per hour, it will go through a steel barricade and not lose any speed. That is momentum. When you push a snowball down a mountain, the further it goes, the more snow it collects, the bigger it becomes and the faster it rolls. It gathers momentum until soon it is unstoppable. There's only one degree difference between the temperatures of hot water and boiling water—just one little degree. That, too, is momentum. And my friends, you never create momentum by stopping and starting. Never.

Consistency is the name of the game. It's one of the biggest keys to success in business. You may not be able to do everything all the time, but you can keep up with the things that are most important. Many of us who are at the top in sales and have been able to stay there for long periods of time are still wives and mothers, and we've proven that it can be done. You can do it, but you have to be consistent.

Once more, the most important principle to realize is that how we perform depends on how we see ourselves. If we're down on ourselves—and it's so easy to get down on ourselves, isn't it?—we will sabotage ourselves and not reach our goal. But if I change the way I see myself and I'm more positive, I'll operate with consistency. I'll feel good about myself, and I'll change my behavior. That will cause me to perform accordingly, and ultimately I'll change my destiny.

WE DON'T REACH OUR GOALS BECAUSE WE FREEZE UP

The final thing I want to mention is that we don't achieve our goals because we get too uptight. We've all been there. We want something so badly we literally let it immobilize us. In sports they call it "choking."

If you put most people in a corner and get them under pressure, they get uptight and become immobilized. The only way I know to avoid this is to concentrate on the effort and not on the results. Just believe with all your heart that if you will consistently put in this effort, the results will be there. Then forget about the results and do the work.

My favorite illustration of this happening is the young

couple trying to get pregnant. You know the story. They try, and they try, and they try some more. They keep temperature charts, they stand on their heads, they do everything the doctor says to do, and nothing happens. Finally they decide, "Enough. We'll adopt a baby." Within a couple of months after they decide to adopt, the woman's pregnant. The physical act didn't change; it's just that the pressure was off. Don't worry about getting the results. If you make the effort consistently, the results will be there.

So learn to be a goal-setter and be driven by your goals. I make it a point to never be without a goal. When I reach one goal, I already have the next one set. If you don't have the next goal waiting in the wings, as soon as you meet your current one, you'll begin to drift. Don't ever let yourself slip into limbo. Don't forget: you can't coast uphill!

The only caution I have is this: don't go to the extreme and get so focused on your goal that you lose sight of what's truly important in life. Your goal may be worthy, but you have to be sure your essential spiritual and social requirements are given appropriate attention. It's upsetting to me when people think that all I do is "eat, sleep, and drink" my business. Not true! I work really hard at having a balance in my life. My priorities are clear. My faith is important to me—the Lord is number one in my life. And I spend lots of time with my family. Fortunately, many of those family activities blend in with my business.

I love my family's involvement in my business. The reason

they're involved is that I've trained them to be. As wives and mothers, we set the tempo in the home. We have to learn to wear many hats. We don't always take this hat off and put the next one on. Sometimes we have about five or six stacked up at once! We're wives, we're mothers, we're Christians, we're citizens, we're chauffeurs, we're bookkeepers, we're lovers, we're cooks—we're at the heart of our families.

Our families and our relationship with the Lord are what are truly important. Goals can help us keep our balance without falling off the edge. The bottom line is that goals are tools to get us where we want to go. Unfortunately, lots of people try to convince themselves they want only what they've got instead of deciding to get what they really want.

CHAPTER 11

Juggling God,
Family, and Work

My biggest piece of advice to women today is simple but brutal: Quit majoring in the minors!

Women are great in the "majors." I would put a lady up against a man any day of the week to slay dragons and kill giants. We're at our best in a crisis. When a kid breaks his leg on the football field, it's mama who's called to come right away. It's mama who's got him loaded in the car rushing him to the emergency room, and it's mama who's sitting up all night to make sure he's all right. Daddy's probably still wandering around the parking lot trying to remember where the car is!

It's the little "dippy" things that really get to us. We lose it when one of the kids is carrying in the groceries, drops the sack, and breaks the two-pound jar of peanut butter. We come unglued, as if it's a matter of life and death, when in fact it isn't going to amount to a hill of beans next week, much less next year.

Do your teenagers' messy bedrooms drive you to the brink? The remedy is simple. Close the door and untwist the light bulb! That way if you're entertaining at night and someone has the audacity to flip the switch, no light comes on. Eddie and I bought our dream home as our children were becoming teenagers. It's a beautiful four-story blue Victorian home. The smartest thing that I did when we moved into that house was put the kids on the fourth floor! No one goes to the fourth floor in my house. You can go up three floors, but then you come to a little rope barring the steps, just like they have in theaters. I have roped off the fourth floor all their lives for two basic reasons.

First, I've always had a lot of events in my home, and I never wanted to be constantly nagging the kids, "Pick up your room—we've got people coming over here tonight." One of the quickest ways to turn your kids off to you and your career is to be on their case all the time.

Second, I didn't want anyone to see where my kids lived. As a teenager, my precious Kim used to walk out of her room with her hair perfect, her clothes spotless, and her makeup flawless. Yet if you looked at her room, you would wonder how she got out of there alive. I never went to the fourth floor; it was just too frustrating!

I've never understood how people could just throw clothes everywhere. Yet my kids never quite learned the difference between the closet and the carpet. Those "c" words tripped them up. I also have never understood how drinking glasses could always go up the stairs but never come down. Our children must have accumulated a full service for eight up there! I'd also find empty shampoo and conditioner bottles in the shower when the trash basket was right outside the shower door. To keep myself from getting upset, I made a conscious choice not to go up there.

Life is frustrating enough as it is. I'm not so stupid as to impose on myself any more frustration than I have to deal with. Sure, we all need to train our kids—and I did. They know how to keep a good house (as adults they have actually turned out quite tidy!). But it wasn't a priority to them at that point in their lives. I could have let myself get an ulcer over it, but instead I chose to close the door.

It's never easy for working moms. I started in direct sales when my kids were little bitty things. I went through every age and every stage with my children while I worked my business. I know what it's like to load the car with the kids, the diaper bag, the pacifiers and changes of clothes—just to drive half a block to buy a loaf of bread. It's an act of Congress!

I also know what it is like to try to get ready to leave for an evening of work. I had to have all my products and samples loaded in the car, have dinner cooked and on the table, and have the baby fed and bathed so Eddie could put him to bed after I got out the door to go to work.

Leaving the kids for any reason can become an emotional liability if you are not careful from the beginning. Has this ever happened to you? You're driving off, and you hear the three-year-old standing there sniffling, with big old tears in his eyes, "Are you leaving me again? I don't ever see you anymore. You're never home." And you feel lower than low. Guess what? *That is exactly how that child wants you to feel.* Make no mistake: kids learn at a very early age how to make you feel guilty. It's not just your kids—it's everybody's kids. Jeff is my eldest, and he is wonderful. He's also a great "travel agent" when it comes to guilt trips. Jeff was always the one who was the free spirit, the non-conformist, the artist and musician. He has a high intellect, is extremely well-read and has a very dry wit. Jeff lived at home until he was twenty-eight years old. (I always said that Jeff wouldn't get married until he was thirty. Sure enough, he got married the year he turned thirty!)

One day I was away at a conference, and Jeff called me and said, "Mom, there's nothing to eat in the house." (Before I go on, you need to understand that my children are all adults now and are our best friends. When we socialize, we automatically want to socialize with our kids. We're more friends than we are parent-child.) Well, when Jeff called and said there wasn't anything to eat, I said, "Jeff, knock it off. I know better." He immediately replied, "Mom, you're right, there is one box of vanilla wafers." I said, "Jeff, you are not going put me on a guilt trip, so don't even try."

"Mother, I'm serious. There's *nothing* to eat. But it's okay. Vanilla wafers really are my favorite cookies. You just go right on and have a good time and don't worry about me. I'll try to manage somehow."

Aren't kids precious? Let me tell you what I've learned about them. From that sniffling little three-year-old to my grown son, everybody wants to know what he is going to get out of it. It's as if all of the members of your family have a little invisible sign hanging around their neck that says, "What's in it for me?" If all your career means is that you've got a phone surgically attached to your ear and you're constantly saying, "Be quiet, go away, I don't have time, not tonight, honey, I've got a headache," then your family is not going to be real excited about your career.

The trick is to figure out how to work *with* them instead of against them. For example, when he was little, one of my boys wanted a tricycle. So we cut the picture of the tricycle out of the catalog and put it on the poster board right along with my goals. I would say, "Sweetheart, every time Mommy holds a product class, I'll put a dollar in your piggy bank for your tricycle."

Trust me on this: *They will load the car for you!* "Bye, Mommy! Have a good time!"

When your kids are happy, you can go off and work without being on a guilt trip. Who's smarter, you or those kids? Women say to me all the time, "But Rena, you don't understand." (Oh, how I love that phrase!) "I have this little two-year-old, and the only time I can get anything done is when Junior takes a nap." Wait a minute. The *mom* is the one who doesn't understand. If she can't control her child's behavior at age two, she's going to be real high on my prayer list when Junior is about fourteen or fifteen. By that time, she is in for some real trouble!

Kids learn early on where the boundaries are. As I said earlier, when I started my career I was living in government housing. My "office" was a card table in the corner of my kitchen with a folding chair and a cardboard box. I was top of my unit for three consecutive years working from a card table, a folding chair and a cardboard box. When I sat down at that table, my kids knew Mommy was working, and they knew not to interrupt me. They had to be bleeding and bleeding badly to come interrupt me.

I was never mean to my kids—don't ever think that. I've got the best rapport that any parent can have. We still have wonderful times. There's rarely a day goes by that I don't see all three of my kids, and they're all adults and married. But, when my kids were young, I taught them *respect*. I would say, "Kiddos, Mommy's going to be working. Now you all go play. When the big hand gets here and the little hand gets here, come get me, and I'll read you that story, I'll push you in the swing, and we'll get ice cream."

Look at the lessons they learned. They learned you have to give up something to gain something, and they learned goal setting. They learned to respect me as a human being and to be independent. They learned how to work together, developing a team spirit. They learned these valuable lessons when they were tiny little things, and now I take great joy in seeing them apply the same principles in their adult lives.

Your kids learn from you. They're always watching you. They even watch how you handle success. Are you arrogant with your success? I feel so sad when I see that happen. Success without humility breeds arrogance.

An incident involving a famous boxer demonstrates just how success can turn someone into an arrogant person. This former heavyweight champion was on a flight one day. He sat in the first class section and, as usual, the flight attendant walked through the cabin instructing everyone to buckle his seat belt. The flight attendant very cordially asked this man to buckle-up for take-off. His reply was, "Superman don't need to buckle up." The flight attendant leaned over to him and said, "Superman don't need no airplane. Buckle up."

Kids don't just watch how you handle success. They also watch how you handle disappointment or failure. Train your children to take all things in stride. Lead by example, teach them respect and give them jobs and chores when they're as young as two years old. Even a two-year-old can straighten pillows on the sofa, pick up books and newspapers and put away toys. Teaching them responsibility at a young age will help balance their perspective so that responsibility doesn't seem oppressive when they are older.

One of the blessings of young children is that they basically stay where you put them. Just wait till they all get to ages ten to sixteen. Wow! You haven't lived until you get to that stage. Everybody's involved in everything and *nobody drives but you!* Like most families, we did it all—piano, guitar, karate, voice lessons, peewee this, little league that. I had three kids playing ball at the same time in three different leagues. That meant practice every day on three different fields and three ball games per week per child—nine ball games a week! Now don't tell me I have to go to nine ball games a week or I'm not being a good mama. That is wrong.

The philosophy of Mary Kay is *God first, family second, and career third.* For those of you who don't know me, you need to know right now nobody loves the Lord more than I do. And nobody is prouder of our philosophy than I am. But this philosophy can be incredibly abused at times. Some people, notably family members, just don't understand what it means when we say *God first, family second, career third.* Let me give you an illustration that may help.

Kim, who was a cheerleader in high school, called me one day and said, "Mama, can you come pick up all of us cheerleaders quick? We've got to be across town in thirty minutes to do a pep rally over at this other school." I said, "Kim, honey, I can't. I have a lady coming over in thirty minutes." "Oh, but Mother you've got to. You're the only mother that doesn't work." Then she went on and on and on. Now, I admit I would have been disappointed in her if she *hadn't* gone on and on since I had trained her practically since birth to persevere and never to take a no personally. She knew that my objection simply meant she hadn't convinced me yet.

Finally she said, "Mother, if you really wanted to, you could find a way over, under, around, or through to help us out." I thought for a moment and said, "You know what, Kim? You're right. I *don't* want to. Sweetheart, may I remind you that my word is my bond? I told that lady that I would be here when she arrives, and I'm going to be here. Now sweetheart, if I had known about your need first (*and here's the key phrase*) I'd have been there because you are more important to me than that lady. But I didn't know about your need. I gave my word, and I'm going to honor it. Now, as good as you are, I'm sure you can find an alternate plan. Just remember how much I love you, and have a good day."

And you know what? They got there without me dropping everything and coming to the rescue!

One day my son Brian called and said, "Mom, I accidentally locked my keys in the car, and the motor's running." He had gone to the cleaners, jumped out, and pushed the automatic locks out of habit. Now in our house we have a place where we keep all the keys in a pile. I got a paper bag, went to the key bin, took all the keys and threw them in the sack. Then I drove to the cleaners and said, "Here are the keys, son. Good luck and God bless."

When Eddie came home that night I told him what had happened. He said, "Sweetheart, why did you take him *all* the keys? Why didn't you take him just the GM keys instead of the house keys, the neighbor's key and Kim's house key?" I said, "Eddie, whose problem was it? It wasn't mine. It was Brian's problem. Brian could figure out which key he needed. And he did."

The principle here is to first identify the problem, and second, decide whose problem it is. Then give it back to whomever it belongs! We often get into messes because we're trying to fix everything. You're trying to solve all your kids' problems, your husband's problems, the neighbors' problems, your brother's and your sister's problems. Quit. Give the problems back to their rightful owners.

Women are the worst at getting over-committed. I think there are two major reasons why this happens. First, they don't have confidence enough to say *no*. Second, they are starved for recognition. When somebody says, "Oh, we need you to be the carnival chairman. You'd be so good, and you'd raise more money than we've ever raised before," they start thinking, they are really needed. "Sure, I'd be glad to do it." Then they end up hopping from one guilt trip to another all their lives.

Part of having a healthy family is recognizing that we can't do it all. As I said earlier, I used to be a seamstress, and I love to sew. But my good business suit once had its main button held on for a whole year with a safety pin! Was it because I didn't know how to sew on a button? Of course not. Was it because I'm too good to sew on a button? No, I'm not above doing anything that is legal, honest, and morally right. I can scrub commodes with the best of 'em!

I didn't take the time to sew the button on because sewing on that button would not have helped me reach my goals in life. There are five areas that I work at constantly—my spiritual life, my family life, my health, building my personal business, and building the company. Understand, too, that each of these areas includes counseling, whether it's marriage counseling, cancer counseling, or helping people. If it doesn't fit in those five areas, I just don't do it. Sewing a button on didn't fit. Now if it had bugged me, I would have paid to have it fixed. But it didn't bug me. That button was fine with a safety pin as far as I was concerned.

Take a few moments to figure out what bugs you. I love having a "bug" list. I write down everything that bugs me. I don't worry about how I'm going to take care of it, I just write it down. After you've made your list, then decide whether you want to fix it yourself or hire someone else to fix it. If it doesn't bug you, don't worry about it. But if it's bugging you, you need to get it taken care of. You either fix it yourself, hire somebody else to fix it, or change your attitude about it.

The principle here is that you cannot be all things to all people. People are appalled that I don't know my mother's phone number by heart. It's on the Rolodex beside my bed, the Rolodex in my office, the Rolodex in my secretary's office, it's in the phone book and the information operator even has it! But people are still aghast that it is not in my head. *It doesn't matter.* I can't find one good reason to memorize her number. What I'm doing works for me!

I don't choose to keep up with politics. In fact, I choose not to spend my time scouting out the best candidate for the position. Eddie enjoys doing that, so he gives me a "cheat sheet" to help me vote. But I don't have enough time to do the research and everything else I need to do. The same principle applies to current events. I couldn't tell you who the hottest star in Hollywood is if my life depended on it. The reason is that knowing current events doesn't help me build my spiritual life, my health, my family, my career, or the company. It's not important for me in reaching my goals. I'm not saying that those things are wrong. I'm simply trying to show you that you have to decide. You have to accept the fact that you can't do it all, and you have to learn to say no without feeling guilty.

I can remember going through a time when I thought, "My poor, precious daughter. I only have one daughter, and I'm not teaching her to sew or knit or crochet. She doesn't know how to do needlepoint or freeze corn or make jelly or pickles. My mama taught me all those things, but I'm not teaching my only daughter. I must be a bad mother."

Then one day I realized that the last thing on earth Kim wanted to learn was how to knit! It's especially difficult for women who are fifty or sixty years old to understand this. We've got more hang-ups than young women have today because we grew up with lots of Cinderella concepts. I will never decoupage again. I will never do crewel embroidery again. It served a time and a purpose in my life, but I have grown past that and it's okay.

One of the ways I kept from feeling guilty was by organizing my home and planning what we did. When my kids were between ten and sixteen years old, I learned the value of "weekly plan sheets." I don't know how anybody lives without weekly plan sheets (but then again I don't know how people live without goals, either!). Our family sat down on Sunday nights after church and planned the coming week.

This especially helped in the summertime when all the kids were home and everybody wanted to do something different. It can drive you crazy! Kim would say, "Susie and I want to go to the swimming pool tomorrow," and Brian would say, "Steve and I want to play miniature golf," and Jeff, of course, wanted to do something no one else had thought of. I would sit down, and I would say, "Okay, Kim, I'm going to drop you and Susie off at the pool at ten, and I'll be back at two. Be wrapped in your towel waiting for me—and no, I'm not coming in to see one more dive. Okay? Brian, I'll take you and Steve to the miniature golf course at nine, and I'll be back at three. You know how to tell time, right, son? Be on the curb waiting. I don't want to have to get out and look for you. And, no, I don't want to have to honk."

We would all sit there and map out the week.

In the middle of the week Brian might ask, "Mom, can we go to the movies?" I'd say, "Brian, is it on the weekly time sheet? It's not? Nope, we're not going. What did you want to see? Oh, that's supposed to be a good movie. I'd like to see that one, too. I tell you what—next Sunday night when we plan next week, remind me. Let's put down a time for you and me to go together; I'd like to see that one with you."

Many women today never schedule any time for enjoying themselves. When do you get a chance to curl up with a good book, go to a movie, or take a friend to lunch? When do you make time for a pedicure? If you don't have it scheduled, you'll suddenly look down and see that there is only one speck of red polish in the middle of your big toe! My advice: when you're organizing your family's time, be sure to reserve some for what *you* want to do.

It breaks my heart to see parents drop everything they're doing and run and cater to their children. That is doing them the biggest injustice in the world. They must be taught responsibility and independence—and they need to be taught by you.

Who calls the shots at your house, you or the kids? When my kids left their lunch money at home, I took it to them the first time. The next time, they did without lunch, or they sold somebody a pencil or an eraser and bought something to eat! But I didn't drop everything I was doing and take lunch to them.

I laugh when I think of all the creative things I used to do when my kids were little. Since I wanted to do phone work on Saturday morning, I used to offer a prize every Friday to whoever slept latest on Saturday morning! When the kids were too little to fix breakfast for themselves, I'd take their cereal bowls and their cereal and set it in front of the television on Friday night. They would get up Saturday morning and watch cartoons and munch their cereal.

The day finally came when they discovered they were supposed to have milk on their cereal (to this day I don't know who told them!). So I began putting milk in a little Tupperware pitcher on the bottom shelf in the refrigerator, and, since they were too little to open the refrigerator by themselves, I tied a rope to the door. With a little teamwork they always managed to get it open. It took some effort, but they got the milk for their cereal, and they didn't have to disturb my work to do it.

What I'm getting at is simply this: I taught them *independence*. I'm sure my cancer played a big part in all of this, but I worked out this system way before that battle. I wanted my kids to be strong and independent and secure. I wanted them to think on their feet and be just fine, whether I was around or not.

I often joke with my family and say, "When I die, don't tell anybody. Just talk as if I'm here, and you can probably collect a check for three years before they know I'm gone!" Now, remember, this is just a joke. The point is that I have my home and my business organized so that everybody has jobs and responsibilities that will be taken care of with or without me.

Training our kids and our family makes them into responsible and considerate adults. That is our responsibility. Remember, we moms set the tempo in the home—for better or for worse.

IF YOU CAN HAVE IT ALL, THEN HOW IN THE WORLD DO YOU MANAGE IT?

I believe you haven't lived until your kids are all over sixteen years of age! Everybody has cars, traffic tickets, fender benders, and everybody locks keys in their cars... of course, with the motor running! Kids are going in a squillion and one directions. My kids always brought home strays—and not just stray animals. They also brought home stray *people*. We had kids constantly moving in, moving out, and going someplace. But I wouldn't have had it any other way. I've always wanted my kids to bring their friends to our house.

When I was a young mother I heard a story that I'll never forget.

One day a little boy was crying as his daddy was yelling at him, saying, "Son, why do you always bring all your friends and play in our yard? Why don't you ever go to somebody else's yard?" You see, that dad's pride and joy was his well-manicured lawn, which now had a place worn out for home plate, first, second, and third base. He continued to yell at his son until the little boy looked up and said, "Daddy, the grass will grow back."

I've never forgotten that story. Eddie and I have always loved for our kids to bring their friends to our house and we still do. We want it that way. We have quite a gym, with state-of-the-art exercise equipment. The kids love to come over and work out. (I'm no dummy!) And the grandkids are already doing the same thing.

I know some people think, "Well, Rena, your kids are all grown, so now you probably don't have any challenges." Think again! When you've got kids, you've got them for life. You grandmothers can appreciate that. My house is still a zoo, and I love it.

WHEN YOUR HOUSE LOOKS
AS IF A BOMB JUST WENT OFF

I firmly believe that lack of organization is the third major contributor to failure in business for many women. Number one is low self-esteem, and number two is lack of self-discipline. Organization doesn't necessarily mean neat or tidy. But there is a thin, thin line between a "cluttered desk that is a sign of genius" and a cluttered desk that can be the cause of a cluttered mind! Organization really means being in control.

Even if my desk is piled high, if you ask me for that list of people for the luncheon tomorrow, I can go right to it. We need to have everything in a certain place and strive to keep it there. Stop and think about that a minute. If you could open the drawers for the Scotch tape or the scissors, and they were always there, wouldn't it be wonderful? We need to teach our families (and ourselves) to put things back where they belong when we are through using them. Not later, but now! When you write up a sales ticket, immediately tear it apart and put each copy where it belongs. It's just a little habit, but it will keep you from facing the weekend with two or more hours of bookwork. We don't want to do bookwork. We're not paper people; we're *people* people.

Organization saves time. Now, don't get me wrong. I don't spend my time alphabetizing my spices! That is a poor use of my time. Why? Because I'm not in control of everybody who's using the spices. When one of the family members comes through and digs through the spices, it's going to get all messed up anyway. That is not the kind of organization I'm talking about.

Open up the drawers in my bathroom vanity, however, and you'll see organization! Every pair of earrings is in a separate cubicle. One day I spent three hours and about forty dollars at a container store. I bought these little plastic trays with little cubicles that fit in the drawers with little cubicles, and I put every pair of earrings together. That was a good use of my time. Not once in the six years that have passed since then have I had to sort through my jewelry trying to match earrings. It used to take forever to find a matching pair. And if the phone was ringing and a child was crying, and I was already late, guess what happened to my attitude? I was a wreck! I was allowing stupid earrings to control my emotions! I would walk out the door in a snit. So taking a few hours and a few dollars to organize my drawers was a good idea. Otherwise, my disorganized jewelry would still be bugging me!

I mentioned earlier about planning the family's time. But if you are going to be organized, you need to plan *your* time, too. Take cooking, for instance. On a weekly plan sheet, plan out your menus for a week at a time on a permanent piece of paper. Do that for a month—just four weeks—and you'll never have to worry about it again. From then on, you can just rotate meals.

Plan ahead for just one week when you're first getting started. When you cook spaghetti sauce, cook extra spaghetti sauce and freeze it. Learn the value of crock-pots. Since we didn't have crock-pots and microwaves when I was young, I had to be "creative." If I came in late and didn't have dinner going, I'd quickly fry an onion. Eddie would walk in the house and say, "Boy, dinner smells good,"—not knowing it was only one fried onion! By the time we sat down to dinner, I would have come up with something, and everyone would be happy!

One thing that is often hard for people to organize or manage is their money, so here's another recommendation. Carry a moneybag in your purse, and all week long get a receipt for everything you do. Immediately write on the back of the receipt—whether you paid cash or wrote a check. Then write down what it was for and put the receipt in the moneybag. Get an accordion file; it's the simplest way in the world to keep your records. Once a week when you empty your bag, throw the receipts in the right category—automobile, office supplies, postage, utilities, food, entertainment and miscellaneous. When the bank statement comes in, take the canceled checks and staple them to the corresponding receipts. (Your CPA will love you if you'll do that every month and have twelve files all ready at the end of the year!)

One of the best ways to be organized is to teach your family to be responsible. They can learn responsibility when they're little, and then everybody shares the load. It's not "mama does it all." When mama does everything, it's an injustice to the family.

Here's my secret to being organized. It's found in the old cliché: "*When I works, I works hard, and when I plays, I plays hard, and when I sits, I sits hard."* I think this is a really important maxim to live by. You have to learn that there are times you can walk out of the house and it's okay that it looks like an atomic bomb went off. Your *house* isn't what is important. Your *home* is what's important.

We all have different priorities during the various seasons of our life. Going to the ball field to see the kids play may be what's important right now. Don't be a perfectionist. Some jobs need to be done better than others. Although we've been taught, "Any job worth doing is worth doing well," it isn't really important whether or not you make the bed every morning. And the days you do make it, it isn't important that it's made perfectly. You might just pull the covers to the top of the bed and go on to the next thing. Every job that is done does not have to be done to the minute detail. Don't ever forget that some things are more important than others are.

You have to give yourself permission not to be perfect. Most of the time, a husband thinks the house is clean if there are no dishes in the sink, the beds are made, and he doesn't have to get out of the car and move toys in order to pull into the garage! Men don't see the cobwebs in the corner. They really don't. The fact that you used a toothbrush to clean the kitchen tile floor goes unnoticed. But does it really matter anyway? Sometimes I ask myself, "If God told me today that I had six weeks to live, what would I do with my time?" I know I would spend time with my family, my parents, and my kids. I would go to church, and I would still sell and hold appointments. But

I know for sure that I wouldn't be worrying about the cobwebs or the kitchen floor. It's a good little test you may want to ask yourself from time to time.

Of course, my advice here is not an excuse to be filthy or sloppy, but to learn to be organized and not to sweat the small stuff. Just learn to close doors and untwist light bulbs and you'll be surprised at how happy you and your family can be!

IT'S TIME TO THROW AWAY THE GUILTS

My heart aches for young mothers today. The reason is that many of them impose all sorts of guilt trips on themselves when they really don't have to. They rob themselves of the joy they could have because they hang on to some of their preconceived ideas about what being a good wife and mother means. You can make your life simpler by cutting out unnecessary traditions. I don't mean essential traditions such as church, of course. It is just that sometimes we do things in a complicated way without even knowing why. Let me give you an illustration of what I mean.

There was a young couple that got married. When the bride went to cook her first ham, she cut the end off the ham before she cooked it. Her husband asked, "Honey, why are you doing that?" She thought for a moment and said, "Mama always does it this way." He looked at her and asked, "Why?" She shrugged her shoulders. "I don't know."

"Call your mother and find out. I'm curious." So she called her mother and asked her, "Mama, how come you always cut the end off the ham before you cook it?" She replied, "Because Grandma always did it that way." The daughter asked, "Why?" Her mother replied, "I don't really know."

"Now I'm really curious," the young groom said. "Let's call Grandma and find out why." So the new bride called her grandmother and asked, "Grandma, how come you always cut the end off the ham before you cook it?" The grandmother said, "Why, honey, it's the only way it'd fit my pan!"

Here we are, three generations later, and we're still cutting the end off the ham. It's silly, isn't it? But it's really human nature. We cling to that which we've been taught without even knowing why. So I'm challenging you to check it out. Be sure that you don't have little things like this holding you back for no good reason. Life's too short not to enjoy it to the fullest!

MAKE SURE YOU
MAKE TIME FOR YOU!

Make the time and schedule the time for *you*. Ask yourself, "Am I making time for myself? Do I have balance in my life?" The answer is either yes or no. There is no "sort of." It's like being "a little bit pregnant"; you either are or you're not!

Let me tell you one more little trick of the trade. When you do have a real problem, a challenge, or situation (whatever you want to call it), realize that it may be something over which you have no control. Perhaps one of your children is struggling for some reason, and it's not something you can fix. I'm not going to sit here and say, "Don't worry about it." We know we're going to be concerned because we love our kids. But there is a positive way to respond to the situation.

St. Francis of Assisi once prayed, "Lord, give me the courage to change the things I can, the patience to accept the things I can't, and the wisdom to know the difference."

When I have a situation that is bothering me, and there is nothing that I can do about it, I know that if I worry about it, it will only hinder me from being my best. When this happens, I play this little game with myself to stop worrying. I write the problem down on a piece of paper, and then I place that problem in the trash. At our house, Eddie collects the garbage in those big, black garbage bags, and when the bag is full, he holds the top of the bag, twists it around, and puts the twisty on it. Then it goes to the garage for the trash man. So I see my worry go out with the garbage.

Now, since I've done it so many times, I can just do this mentally. In my mind, I hold the top of the bag, twist it around, put the twisty on it, and I'll carry it out to the garage. What I am saying to myself is, "I cannot deal with this right now emotionally, and I've got other things to do. I'll put it right out here; I know exactly where it is, and when I'm ready to deal with it and spend some more thought or time on it, I'll go back and get it. But I don't have to deal with it right now."

Silly little game, isn't it? But I'm telling you, it works!

Sometimes we have to decide *not* to decide what to do with a problem. We put it in a trash bag and put it over there to one side until it's time to make that decision. Then we are free to do what we need to do at the moment.

HOW PUTTING EACH OTHER FIRST MAKES A SUCCESSFUL MARRIAGE

One of the tragic things I see today in many marriages is that too often the kids come before the husband. But here's the plain truth: your husband must come *before* your kids. I know a lot of men who are married to a wonderful mommy and a not-so-wonderful wife. And we wonder why so many married men are having extramarital affairs! Remember, you are your husband's partner, and he can't come in second, even if it's a close second. Relationships don't just happen—they take work.

We need to spend time with the people we love, for we fall in love with the people we spend time with. That is the reason doctors fall in love with nurses, and bosses fall in love with secretaries. They spend more time with the people at work than they do with their family. Ladies, you need to consciously work at spending time with just *your man*.

Does this mean kids aren't as important? Absolutely not! But the relationship is different. It makes kids very insecure to know that they come before daddy or mommy. They need to know that their parents are committed to each other and that the kids are not running the show.

Each of your children needs you and needs you in different ways. Consciously work at spending time with your children individually. Believe me, they will feel very special.

I've taken each of my kids, one at a time, to different places with me, even after they were married. I had the privilege of throwing out the first ball at the San Francisco Giants game a few years ago when I took Brian, an avid baseball player, to San Francisco. His wife Jill didn't go. Eddie didn't go. Just Brian and I went, and we had a ball—no pun intended! My son escorted me to the mound and sat on the sidelines as his mother totally embarrassed him with her pitch! He hung out in the dugout and had the time of his life . . . an experience he'll never forget!

A few years ago, Kim and I went to Acapulco for five days for a little "R & R" and fun in the sun. I've taken Kim and Jill (one of my daughters-in-law) to New York at Christmastime. We rode the carriage in Central Park, saw *Cats* on Broadway, went to see the Rockettes Christmas Show, and had brunch at Tavern on the Green. Jeff's favorite place is Key West, Florida. That's because we spent special times together there. We made memories that are very precious. You can never sit back and put your relationships on "auto pilot." You always have to work at them, but the dividends of your investment will pay off handsomely.

Many women have a hard time balancing a career and a husband. I am often asked, "What do you do when you're married to a negative man?" Well, first off, the bulk of the problem is often *your* fault. Now I know you don't want to hear that, but let me explain why it's true.

We women are very bad about coming home and complaining, or as we say in my house, "dumping garbage." More often than we would all care to admit, we come in and share the negative, and we fail to share the positive. As soon as we see our husband we say something like, "You know, I drove a hundred and fifty miles, and I only made a five-dollar sale." I know it happens because I've done it myself. Our husbands have been taught since they were little boys to be protective. So when he hears you complain, he bristles, and then he says, "Honey, you don't have to put up with that. I make a good living. I'll take care of you."

We then say, "You've never really wanted me to do this, have you?" If he doesn't say anything, we say, "You don't care about my career; all you care about is your own." Poor guy, he can't win! Remember, in his heart, his intent was to protect you. He doesn't know what to do to make you feel better.

Another thing we're often guilty of is comparing him to another man. "You know, dear, if you'd help me with the kids and the dishes and help around the house like Susie's husband does, I'd be more successful, too." Ladies, don't ever compare your man to another man! Do you want to be compared to another woman? I don't! Remember, if he were perfect, he probably wouldn't have married you!

One of the other reasons men can be negative about their wives' careers—if indeed they are—is that they may be thinking, "Show me the money!" If you're working in commission sales, and you're not selling, there's a problem. There *isn't* any money. You probably promised him when you got into business that you were going to "supplement the family's income," or something like that. And he's saying, "All your business has done so far is cost me. I haven't seen any money yet."

I can assure you that when you can say to your husband, "Don't worry about the car payments—I've got them both made this month," or "Honey, don't worry about the house payment, I've got it covered," his attitude will be *very* different. When it's Monday night, and you're starting off to your sales meeting, he isn't going to say, "Are you going to another one of those stupid meetings?" No, not at all. He'll probably walk you to your car and give you a big kiss!

One of the top saleswomen I know got up one year at our conference and said (I just love this!), "I made my husband a deal when I got into business. I promised him that every time I held a class, we'd make love. You know, I've *never* had a problem with him being supportive of my business." She went on to say, "Every Monday morning, he's the first to say, 'Honey, how many classes have you got booked this week?'"

Now you might laugh, but she's one of the top saleswomen in the entire nation! You see, she knew he was wearing that little invisible sign that says, "What's in it for me?"

Many times the problem is that men are afraid that you are going to become so successful and independent that you'll no longer need them. There are many insecure men in this world, just as there are many insecure women. We need to help build that self-esteem in them, too. We should always focus on building them up rather than tearing them down.

I've often remarked what a difference it would make if we would treat our men as we treat new business associates. When we're working with someone new and she makes a mistake, we say, "No problem. You know I'm here to help you. That's how we learn." When our men make mistakes, however, what do we say? "You idiot, I cannot believe that you..." We seem to feel obligated to remind him over and over and over how far short he falls of perfection!

The best way to keep a healthy relationship is to remember to treat the other person the way you would want to be treated. There's no expiration date on the Golden Rule.

CHAPTER 12

Reach for Success!

My battle with cancer began in 1975 with my first mastectomy. But even though it's been an ongoing battle with numerous surgeries and untold amounts of therapy, I have done my best and most creative work during this time, as well as raised my children into happy, productive adults who've given me wonderful grandchildren. I share this because we all tend to wonder in difficult situations whether we can continue to work and advance in our profession and still have "normal" lives.

The answer is yes! I believe with all my heart that regardless of the obstacles, problems, frustrations and disappointments in life, *it's not what happens to us but how we respond to it that counts.*

Have my challenges with cancer ended? Not yet. In June 1996, they discovered cancer in my skull, and I started chemotherapy again.

Of course I would never have chosen to have cancer (as if

we were given choices in these matters). But I can honestly say I am a stronger, better person on account of having to face the challenge of living with cancer. I've learned how to make it work as a positive force in my life. It has taught me to make the most out of every situation. And it has also repeatedly turned me to the Lord. I fully realize that in and of myself I couldn't have made it this far.

A number of years ago, there was an Olympic marathon runner who, due to a pulled hamstring, finished five and one-half hours after the last person had finished the race. When he finally crossed the finish line, a few reporters were hanging around waiting to interview him. They curiously asked, "Why did you even bother to complete the course?" The young man quietly replied, "My country did not send me here to start the race. My country sent me here to *finish* the race."

No matter what your goal, my challenge to you is to run and not give in, give up, or give out until you've crossed that finish line. Oh, you'll get weary, you'll get discouraged, and you'll have setbacks. Some days it's three steps forward and two steps back. Some days it's just two steps forward and three steps back. But no matter what, it is always too soon to quit. *When you keep your goal in sight, quitting is never an option.*

The people I admire most in this world are those who keep on trying *regardless* of the obstacles they face. When we have done our very best, we can hold our head high and be proud. Doing our best is the true measure of success. When you do this, you'll learn that you really can live, and laugh, and love your way to a more fulfilling, successful, and rewarding life.

There is a poem I have come to love deeply. I've shared this with many of my friends and I would like to share it with you. This poem has been a source of encouragement to me in difficult times over the years. And it's my prayer that it will encourage you to "keep on keeping on" as you continue to push forward to *your* finish line.

"The Race"

"Quit! Give up! You're beaten!"
They shout out and plead.
"There's just too much against you now.
This time you can't succeed!"

And as I start to hang my head
In front of failure's face,
My downward fall is broken by
The memory of a race.

And hope refills my weakened will
As I recall that scene;
For just the thought of that short race
Rejuvenates my being.

A children's race—young boys, young men;
How I remember it well.
Excitement, sure, but also fear;
It wasn't hard to tell.

They all lined up so full of hope;
Each thought to win that race.
Or tie for first, or if not that,
At least take second place.

And fathers watched from off the side,
Each cheering for his son.
And each boy hoped to show his dad
That he would be the one.

The whistle blew and off they went!
Young hearts and hopes afire.
To win, to be the hero there
Was each young boy's desire.

And one boy in particular
Whose dad was in the crowd,
Was running near the lead and thought
"My dad will be so proud."

But as he sped down the field
Across a shallow dip,
The little boy who thought to win
Lost his step and slipped.

Trying hard to catch himself
His hands flew out to brace,
Amid the laughter of the crowd
He fell flat on his face.

So down he fell and with him hope—
He couldn't win it now—
Embarrassed, sad, he only wished
That he could disappear somehow.

But as he fell, his dad stood up
And showed his anxious face,
Which to the boy so clearly said:
"Get up and win that race!"

He quickly rose, no damage done
Behind a bit, that's all
And ran with all his mind and might
To make up for his fall

So anxious to restore himself,
To catch up and to win
His mind went faster than his legs;
He slipped and fell again!

He wished that he had quit before
With only one disgrace.
"I'm hopeless as a runner now;
I shouldn't try to race."

But in the laughing crowd he searched
And found his father's face.
That steady look that said again:
"Get up and win that race!"

So he jumped up to try again.
Ten yards behind the last–
"If I'm going to gain those yards," he thought,
"I've got to run real fast."

Exerting everything he had,
He gained eight or ten,
But trying so hard to catch the lead
He slipped and fell again!

Defeat! He lay there silently
A tear dropped from his eye—
"There's no sense running anymore:
Three strikes I'm out, why try?"

The will to rise had disappeared
All hope had fled away;
So far behind, so error-prone:
A loser all the way.

"I've lost, so what's the use," he thought.
"I'll live with my disgrace."
But then he thought about his dad
Who soon he'd have to face.

"Get up," an echo sounded low,
"Get up and take your place.
You were not meant for failure here.
Get up and win that race."

With borrowed will, "Get up," it said,
"You haven't lost at all,
For winning is not more than this:
To rise each time you fall."

So up he rose to win once more,
And with a new commit
He resolved that win or lose,
At least he wouldn't quit.

So far behind the others now.
The most he'd ever been—
Still he gave it all he had
He ran as though to win.

Three times he had fallen stumbling:
Three times he rose again.
Too far behind to hope to win
He still ran to the end.

They cheered the winning runner
As he crossed first place,
Head high and proud and happy;
No falling, no disgrace.

But when the fallen youngster
Crossed the line last place,
The crowd gave him the greater cheer
For finishing the race.

And even though he came in last
With head bowed low, unproud,
You would have thought he'd won the race
To listen to the crowd.

And to his dad he sadly said,
"I didn't do so well."
"To me you won," his father said.
"You rose each time you fell."

And you know when things seem dark and hard
And difficult to face,
The memory of that little boy
Helps me in my race.

For all of life is like that race.
With ups and downs and all.
All you have to do to win
Is rise each time you fall.

"Quit! Give up, you're beaten!"
They still shout in my face.
But another voice within me says:
"GET UP AND WIN THAT RACE!"

—Author Unknown

RENA'S RECOMMENDATIONS

Rena Tarbet's

Circle of Hope

An Inspiring Video on How To Take Back
Your Life and Win the Struggle with Cancer

Rena Tarbet's medical story is not that different from many. She faced cancer and the many following complications when she least expected it. What is different about her story is her choice of attitude, lifestyle, medicine, and faith that provided the strength and motivation to conquer it.

This one hour and fifteen minute video explores the many facets of cancer and specific ways cancer patients, along with their friends and families, can cope with this deadly disease. Rena speaks candidly and from the heart with comments from her doctor, the nurse that worked with her during her treatments, her closests friends, and her husband and children. As Rena tells her own story, you will be encouraged by her response to this disease and her answers to the toughest questions many people face when confronted with the news of cancer.

Rena shares from her own experience how to develop a positive self-esteem regardless of health challenges and how to take control of your destiny. Rena also shares exactly how to take advantage of every means available to live your life to the fullest, realizing it is not just what happens to us that matters, but how we deal with it!

Here's what others have said about Rena's *Circle of Hope* video:

"If you, a friend, or a member of your family is facing cancer, I know you, too, will find this video a true source of inspiration." Mary Kay Ash

"Rena has a message of hope and encouragement . . . she deals with the physical, mental, spiritual, and support side of the cancer battle." Zig Ziglar

"This video has so much to offer—it should be required reading for every cancer patient and every medical professional." Julie Hise, cancer survivor

To order Rena's *Circle of Hope* video, please send payment of $25 plus $3.95 for postage and handling at the address below. You can charge your purchase to Visa or MasterCard (Please include the card number and expiration date along with your name, address, city, state and zip code, and daytime telephone number.) All checks should be made payable to J&J Productions. For faster service, call toll-free 1-800-467-4808. We are pleased that a portion of all profits from the sale of these videos go to reaching out to cancer patients and their families for a better quality of life today. Please mail your request to:

Rena's *Circle of Hope* Video
c/o J&J Productions
P.O. Box 211945 • Bedford, TX 76095-8945